SHARED
LEADERSHIP

SHARED LEADERSHIP

The Roles and Functions of Apostolic Teams in Establishing True Apostolic Church Government in the Local Church

Dr. John A. Tetsola

Shared Leadership

The Roles and Functions of Apostolic Teams in Establishing True Apostolic Church Government in the Local Church

ISBN 1-929620-03-9

Note: In some Scripture quotations, italics have been added by the author for emphasis only.

Table of Contents

CHAPTER I

THE ELDERSHIP MINISTRY IN THE LOCAL CHURCH

Therefore, I exhort the elders among you, as your fellow elder and witness of the sufferings of Christ,

shepherd the flock of God among you, exercising oversight not under compulsion, but voluntarily, according to the will of God;

I Peter 5:1a, 2a NASB

Often when we hear about eldership, we think of them as officials of the church board, influential people within the local church or even advisers to the pastor. We think of them as fundraisers or mere administrators. We don't expect them to teach and preach the word of truth and to be intricately involved in the shepherding of the people. This conception is completely wrong. One does not need to be professionally trained in theology to understand that this concept of eldership is irreconcilably at odds with the New Testament definition of eldership.

According to the New Testament concept of eldership, elders lead the church, teach and preach the Word, protect the church from false teachers, exhort and admonish the saints in sound doctrine, visit the sick and pray, and judge doctrinal issues. In biblical terminology, elders shepherd, oversee, lead and care for the local church.

> **Be on guard for yourselves and for all the flock, among which the Holy Spirit has made you overseers, to shepherd the church of God which He purchased with His own blood.**

Acts 20:28 NASB

> **shepherd the flock of God among you, exercising oversight not under compulsion, but voluntarily, according to the will of God; and not for sordid gain, but with eagerness;**

I Peter 5:2 NASB

Paul reminds the Asian elders that God the Holy Spirit placed them in the flock as overseers for the purpose of shepherding the church of God and Peter exhorts the elders to be all that shepherds should be to the flock. The biblical image of a shepherd caring for his flock is very precious. It is the image of standing for long hours, ensuring the safety of the flock, leading it to fresh pasture and clear water, carrying the weak, seeking the lost, healing the wounded and the sick. The whole image of the Palestinian shepherd is characterized by intimacy, tenderness, concern, skill, hard work, suffering and love. That is why, when Paul and Peter directly exhorted the elders to do their duty, these two apostles employed shepherding imagery. These two great apostles assigned the task of shepherding the local church to no other group or single person but to the elders. Eldership teams today are to be primarily shepherds of a flock and not corporate executives, CEOs or advisers to the pastors. They participate in the corporate shepherding of the flock with the set man or the senior minister.

Although the term "elder" is the predominant New Testament term used to describe local church leaders and is especially suited to the nature of the New Testament churches, it conveys to the overwhelming majority of Christians and non-Christians today ideas that are different from those found in the New Testament. A true biblical eldership is not a business-like committee. It is a biblically qualified council of men that JOINTLY pastor the local church.

The New Testament uses a term other than elder to describe local church leaders. That term is "overseer" and it comes from the Greek word *episkopos*. The term "overseer" was a common designation used by the Greeks for a variety of officials. In contrast to all priestly titles, nothing in the title overseer (or elder) violated the local church's family character, humble-servant nature or priestly status. The fact that the apostles and first Christians used the term "overseer" as a synonym for elder demonstrates flexibility in the use of leadership terminology and the desire to communicate effectively among Greek speaking people.

It is very important and critical for Christians today to understand that the language we use to describe our church leaders has the power to accurately reflect biblical thinking and practice or, conversely, to lead us far away from the true Church of Jesus Christ and into the false church.

The term *episkopos* (overseer), for example, developed a meaning that was quite different from the New Testament usage. It became one of the most significant ecclesiastical titles of the hierarchical church. We know that the term in English is "bishop," meaning a church official who presides over many churches and the lower clergy. Thus, the original sense of the term *episkopos*, which was synonymous with elder, indicated a local church official.

If we choose to use the term "elder," which many Protestant churches do because it is a key biblical term for church leaders, it is very necessary to explain that the term "elder" means "pastor elders," "shepherd elders," or "pastors." They are not just board members without shepherding or pastoral responsibilities. Whatever terminology you choose to describe local church leaders will have advantages and disadvantages. In the end, every local church is responsible to teach its people the meaning of the terms it uses to describe its spiritual leaders, whether it be elders, overseers, ministers, preachers or pastors. Biblically sensitive church leaders will insist that the terminology they use represents as accurately as possible the original biblical terms and concepts of a New Testament eldership. The vocabulary Christians use to describe their church officials has great problems. Much of our church vocabulary is unscriptural and terribly misleading. Words such as clergyman, layman, reverend, priest, and bishop convey ideas contrary to what Jesus Christ and His apostles taught.

The Eldership Team

Let the elders who rule well be considered worthy of double honor, especially those who work hard at preaching and teaching.

I Timothy 5:17 NASB

The principle of an eldership team is the principle of sharing the burden and the responsibility of pastoring or shepherding people. It is a "shared" form of leadership. Even though it is a team, there is always a chosen or selected set man or senior elder that heads the team. The pastoral oversight of the apostolic churches was a team effort and not the sole responsibility of one person.

The Model of an Eldership Team

And it came about the next day that Moses sat to judge the people, and the people stood about Moses from the morning until the evening.

Now when Moses' father-in-law saw all that he was doing for the people, he said, "What is this thing that you are doing for the people? Why do you alone sit as judge and all the people stand about you from morning until evening?"

And Moses said to his father-in-law, "Because the people come to me to inquire of God.

When they have a dispute, it comes to me, and I judge between a man and his neighbor, and make known the statutes of God and His laws.

And Moses' father-in-law said to him, "The thing that you are doing is not good.

You will surely wear out, both yourself and these people who are with you, for the task is too heavy for you; you cannot do it alone.

Now listen to me: I shall give you counsel, and God be with you. You be the people's representative before God, and you bring the disputes to God,

then teach them the statutes and the laws, and make known to them the way in which they are to walk, and the work they are to do.

Furthermore, you shall select out of all the people able men who fear God, men of truth, those who hate dishonest gain; and you shall place these over them, as leaders of thousands, of hundreds, of fifties and of tens.

And let them judge the people at all times; and let it
be that every major dispute they will bring to you,
but every minor dispute they themselves will judge.
So it will be easier for you, and they will bear the
burden with you.

If you do this thing and God so commands you, then
you will be able to endure, and all these people also
will go to their place in peace.

Exodus 18:13-23 NASB

Now the people became like those who complain of
adversity in the hearing of the LORD; and when the
LORD heard it, His anger was kindled, and the fire
of the LORD burned among them and consumed
some of the outskirts of the camp.

Then I will come down and speak with you there,
and I will take of the Spirit who is upon you, and
will put Him upon them; and they shall bear the
burden of the people with you, so that you shall not
bear it all alone.

Numbers 11:1, 17 NASB

For I do not want you to be unaware, brethren, that
our fathers were all under the cloud, and all passed
through the sea;

and all were baptized into Moses in the cloud and in
the sea;

and all ate the same spiritual food;

and all drank the same spiritual drink, for they were
drinking from a spiritual rock which followed them;
and the rock was Christ.

Nevertheless, with most of them God was not
well-pleased; for they were laid low in the
wilderness.

> **Now these things happened as examples for us, that we should not crave evil things, as they also craved.**

I Corinthians 10:1-6 NASB

An eldership team is not a new concept. It is rooted in the Old Testament institution of the elders of Israel and in Jesus' founding of the apostolate. Jesus did not appoint one man to lead His Church. He personally appointed and trained twelve men. Jesus Christ gave the Church plurality of leadership. The Twelve comprised the first leadership council of the Church and, in the most exemplary way, jointly led and taught the first Christian community. The Twelve provide a marvelous example of unity, humility, brotherly love and shared leadership structure.

> **But select from among you, brethren, seven men of good reputation, full of the Spirit and of wisdom, whom we may put in charge of this task.**
>
> **But we will devote ourselves to prayer, and to the ministry of the word.**
>
> **And the statement found approval with the whole congregation; and they chose Stephen, a man full of faith and of the Holy Spirit, and Philip, Prochorus, Nicanor, Timon, Parmenas and Nicolas, a proselyte from Antioch.**
>
> **And these they brought before the apostles; and after praying, they laid their hands on them.**

Acts 6:3-6 NASB

A leadership team with shared responsibility is also evidenced by the seven who were appointed to relieve the twelve apostles of the responsibility of dispensing funds to the church's widows. The seven were the prototype of the later

7

deacons. As a body of servants, they did their work on behalf of the church in Jerusalem. In the New Testament, the pastoral oversight of many of the first churches was committed to a plurality of elders. Some of the examples of such pastoral responsibilities are as follows:

Responsibility to the Sick

Is anyone among you sick? Let him call for the elders of the church, and let them pray over him, anointing him with oil in the name of the Lord;

James 5:14 NASB

■ James instructed the sick believer to "call for the elders (plural) of the church (singular)."

And some men came down from Judea and began teaching the brethren, "Unless you are circumcised according to the custom of Moses, you cannot be saved.

And when Paul and Barnabas had great dissension and debate with them, the brethren determined that Paul and Barnabas and certain others of them should go up to Jerusalem to the apostles and elders concerning this issue.

Therefore, being sent on their way by the church, they were passing through both Phoenicia and Samaria, describing in detail the conversion of the Gentiles, and were bringing great joy to all the brethren.

And when they arrived at Jerusalem, they were received by the church and the apostles and the elders, and they reported all that God had done with them.

> But certain ones of the sect of the Pharisees who had believed, stood up, saying, It is necessary to circumcise them, and to direct them to observe the Law of Moses.
>
> And the apostles and the elders came together to look into this matter.
>
> **Acts 15:1-6 NASB**

■ The elders of the church in Jerusalem united with the twelve apostles to deliberate over doctrinal controversy. Like the apostolate, the elders comprised a collective leadership body.

Farewell Exhortation

> And from Miletus he sent to Ephesus and called to him the elders of the church.
>
> Be on guard for yourselves and for all the flock, among which the Holy Spirit has made you overseers, to shepherd the church of God which He purchased with His own blood.
>
> **Acts 20:17, 28 NASB**

> Let the elders who rule well be considered worthy of double honor, especially those who work hard at preaching and teaching.
>
> **I Timothy 5:17 NASB**

■ When passing near the city of Ephesus during a hurried trip to Jerusalem, Paul summoned the "elders of the church," not the pastor, to meet for a final farewell exhortation. The church at Ephesus was under the pastoral care of a council of elders. I Timothy 5:17 demonstrates clearly that a plurality of elders led and taught in Ephesus.

The Overseers

Paul and Timothy, bond-servants of Christ Jesus, to all the saints in Christ Jesus who are in Philippi, including the overseers and deacons:

Philippians 1:1 NASB

■ When Paul wrote to the Christians at Philippi, he greeted "the overseers (plural) and deacons."

Council of Elders

And when they had appointed elders for them in every church, having prayed with fasting, they commended them to the Lord in whom they had believed.

Acts 14:23 NASB

■ At the end of Paul's first missionary journey, he appointed a council of elders for each newly founded church.

Caring for Churches

For this reason I left you in Crete, that you might set in order what remains, and appoint elders in every city as I directed you,

Titus 1:5 NASB

■ At both the beginning and end of Paul's ministry, he appointed (or instructed others to appoint) a plurality of elders to care for the churches he founded or established. Paul did not consider a church to be fully developed until it had functioning, qualified elders: "for this reason I left you in Crete, that you might set in order what remains, and appoint in every city as I directed you."

On the local church level, the New Testament plainly witnesses to a consistent pattern of shared pastoral leadership. Therefore, leadership by a plurality of elders is a sound biblical practice.

Should Women Be Elders Today?

the older women as mothers, and the younger women as sisters, in all purity.

I Timothy 5:2 NASB

Older women likewise are to be reverent in their behavior, not malicious gossips, nor enslaved to much wine, teaching what is good,

Titus 2:3 NASB

There is a great controversy in the Church whether or not women should or should not be elders. There are members who have left churches because of the appointment of women elders and there are those who have continually resisted authority because a woman is placed as an elder over them. There is the Greek word *presbutes*. This word is the female form of the same Greek word *presbuteros* and this word is used several times in Scripture and is usually translated "older women" in our English bible. These women are called to have a motherly function in the church.

In the two major biblical passages on the requirements of elders in I Timothy 3:1-7 and Titus 1:5-9, the Scriptures are clearly talking about men in particular and calling them to a role of fatherhood in the church. Women cannot function effectively as fathers, but the church badly needs mothers as well as fathers. The two roles are not the same and should not be confused. Church life is greatly enriched when wise, mature older women become a part of the eldership and function as mothers in the church. However, we must recognize the distinctive role of fathers and the need to have a clear father or head as the ultimate leader or pastor.

CHAPTER II

TRUE APOSTOLIC STRUCTURE

**For this reason I left you in Crete, that you might set
in order what remains, and appoint elders in every
city as I directed you,**

Titus 1:5 NASB

For many Christians, the issue of the government of the
Church is not important. However Church government is an
extremely practical and theologically important issue. Some
of the disasters that have been created in Christendom have
been the result of unscriptural forms of Church structure.
Church government matters because it determines how people
think and act. It determines how things are done in a local
church. The government of the Church is run by a plurality
of elders. The role of elders is very important in the
government of the Church. The local church is not a one-man
show. It is a corporate show. The government of the local
church is not run by one man, but it is run and governed by a
corporate eldership with a set man or a presiding elder in
charge of the team.

The New Testament records evidence of oversight by a council of elders in nearly all of the first churches. The local churches were spread over a wide geographic and culturally diverse area – from Jerusalem to Rome. Let us look at a couple of examples.

> **And this they did, sending it in charge of Barnabas and Saul to the elders.**
>
> **Acts 11:30 NASB**

> **Is anyone among you sick? Let him call for the elders of the church, and let them pray over him, anointing him with oil in the name of the Lord;**
>
> **and the prayer offered in faith will restore the one who is sick, and the Lord will raise him up, and if he has committed sins, they will be forgiven him.**
>
> **James 5:14-15 NASB**

■ Elders were found in the churches of Judea and the surrounding area.

> **And when Paul and Barnabas had great dissension and debate with them, the brethren determined that Paul and Barnabas and certain others of them should go up to Jerusalem to the apostles and elders concerning this issue.**
>
> **Therefore, being sent on their way by the church, they were passing through both Phoenicia and Samaria, describing in detail the conversion of the Gentiles, and were bringing great joy to all the brethren.**
>
> **And when they arrived at Jerusalem, they were received by the church and the apostles and the elders, and they reported all that God had done with them.**

But certain ones of the sect of the Pharisees who had believed, stood up, saying, It is necessary to circumcise them, and to direct them to observe the Law of Moses.

And the apostles and the elders came together to look into this matter.

And after there had been much debate, Peter stood up and said to them, Brethren, you know that in the early days God made a choice among you, that by my mouth the Gentiles should hear the word of the gospel and believe.

Acts 15:2-7 NASB

■ Elders governed the church in Jerusalem.

And when they had appointed elders for them in every church, having prayed with fasting, they commended them to the Lord in whom they had believed.

Acts 14:23 NASB

And from Miletus he sent to Ephesus and called to him the elders of the church.

Acts 20:17 NASB

It is a trustworthy statement: if any man aspires to the office of overseer, it is a fine work he desires to do.

An overseer, then, must be above reproach, the husband of one wife, temperate, prudent, respectable, hospitable, able to teach,

not addicted to wine or pugnacious, but gentle, uncontentious, free from the love of money.

He must be one who manages his own household well, keeping his children under control with all dignity

(but if a man does not know how to manage his own household, how will he take care of the church of God?);

and not a new convert, lest he become conceited and fall into the condemnation incurred by the devil.

And he must have a good reputation with those outside the church, so that he may not fall into reproach and the snare of the devil.

I Timothy 3:1-7 NASB

Let the elders who rule well be considered worthy of double honor, especially those who work hard at preaching and teaching.

For the Scripture says, YOU SHALL NOT MUZZLE THE OX WHILE HE IS THRESHING, and The laborer is worthy of his wages.

Do not receive an accusation against an elder except on the basis of two or three witnesses.

Those who continue in sin, rebuke in the presence of all, so that the rest also may be fearful of sinning.

I solemnly charge you in the presence of God and of Christ Jesus and of His chosen angels, to maintain these principles without bias, doing nothing in a spirit of partiality.

Do not lay hands upon anyone too hastily and thus share responsibility for the sins of others; keep yourself free from sin.

No longer drink water exclusively, but use a little wine for the sake of your stomach and your frequent ailments.

The sins of some men are quite evident, going before them to judgment; for others, their sins follow after.

Likewise also, deeds that are good are quite evident, and those which are otherwise cannot be concealed.

I Timothy 5:17-25 NASB

Paul and Timothy, bond-servants of Christ Jesus, to all the saints in Christ Jesus who are in Philippi, including the overseers and deacons:

Philippians 1:1 NASB

For this reason I left you in Crete, that you might set in order what remains, and appoint elders in every city as I directed you,

Titus 1:5 NASB

■ Among the Pauline churches, leadership by the plurality of elders was established in the churches of Derbe, Lystra, Iconium and Antioch, in the church at Ephesus, in the church at Philippi and in the churches on the island of Crete.

Peter, an apostle of Jesus Christ, to those who reside as aliens, scattered throughout Pontus, Galatia, Cappadocia, Asia, and Bithynia, who are chosen

I Peter 1:1 NASB

Therefore, I exhort the elders among you, as your fellow elder and witness of the sufferings of Christ, and a partaker also of the glory that is to be revealed,

I Peter 5:1 NASB

■   According to the well-traveled letter of I Peter, elders existed in churches throughout northwestern Asia Minor, Pontus, Galatia, Cappadocia, Asia and Bithynia.

Despite all of these evidences of plurality of elders in the early church, most Christians believe that Timothy, Epaphras and James were the local pastoral leadership– leadership by one individual. That is not true. Timothy was not a local church pastor in the traditional sense of the term. He was primarily an apostolic delegate. He served as Paul's partner in spreading the gospel and strengthening the various churches under Paul's care. Like Timothy, Epaphras was also Paul's apostolic delegate. He ministered on Paul's behalf in the Lycus valley while Paul resided in Ephesus (Colossians 1:2).

> But I did not see any other of the apostles except James, the Lord's brother.
>
> **Galatians 1:19 NASB**
>
> and recognizing the grace that had been given to me, James and Cephas and John, who were reputed to be pillars, gave to me and Barnabas the right hand of fellowship, that we might go to the Gentiles, and they to the circumcised.
>
> **Galatians 2:9 NASB**

James was an apostle who ministered uniquely to the Jews. Along with Peter and John, James was considered one of the "pillars" of the church – not the "pillar." He was one of the most prominent leaders among the leaders in the church at Jerusalem and among all Jewish Christians. Nevertheless, the New Testament never clearly identifies his official position in the church at Jerusalem.   The pastoral and organizational oversight of the local church is to be in the hands of a plurality of qualified elders, not only one person.

Instructions about Biblical Elders

Not only did the New Testament provide examples of elder-led churches, it also includes explicit instructions to churches about how these elders need to be cared for, protected, disciplined, selected, restored and obeyed. The apostles intended that these instructions be obeyed and should be a format for teachings for all of the churches.

> **Is anyone among you sick? Let him call for the elders of the church, and let them pray over him, anointing him with oil in the name of the Lord;**
>
> **James 5:14 NASB**

James instructs those who are sick to call for the elders of the church.

> **Let the elders who rule well be considered worthy of double honor, especially those who work hard at preaching and teaching.**
>
> **For the Scripture says, YOU SHALL NOT MUZZLE THE OX WHILE HE IS THRESHING, and The laborer is worthy of his wages.**
>
> **I Timothy 5:17-18 NASB**

Paul instructs the Ephesian church to financially support elders who labor "at preaching and teaching."

Do not receive an accusation against an elder except on the basis of two or three witnesses.

Those who continue in sin, rebuke in the presence of all, so that the rest also may be fearful of sinning.

I solemnly charge you in the presence of God and of Christ Jesus and of His chosen angels, to maintain these principles without bias, doing nothing in a spirit of partiality.

Do not lay hands upon anyone too hastily and thus share responsibility for the sins of others; keep yourself free from sin.

I Timothy 5:19-22 NASB

■   Paul instructs the local church about protecting elders from false accusation, disciplining elders who sin, and restoring fallen elders.

It is a trustworthy statement: if any man aspires to the office of overseer, it is a fine work he desires to do.

An overseer, then, must be above reproach, the husband of one wife, temperate, prudent, respectable, hospitable, able to teach,

not addicted to wine or pugnacious, but gentle, uncontentious, free from the love of money.

He must be one who manages his own household well, keeping his children under control with all dignity

(but if a man does not know how to manage his own household, how will he take care of the church of God?);

and not a new convert, lest he become conceited and fall into the condemnation incurred by the devil.

And he must have a good reputation with those outside the church, so that he may not fall into reproach and the snare of the devil.

I Timothy 3:1-7 NASB

For this reason I left you in Crete, that you might set in order what remains, and appoint elders in every city as I directed you,

namely, if any man be above reproach, the husband of one wife, having children who believe, not accused of dissipation or rebellion.

For the overseer must be above reproach as God's steward, not self-willed, not quick-tempered, not addicted to wine, not pugnacious, not fond of sordid gain,

but hospitable, loving what is good, sensible, just, devout, self-controlled,

holding fast the faithful word which is in accordance with the teaching, that he may be able

both to exhort in sound doctrine and to refute those who contradict.

Titus 1:5-9 NASB

■ Paul instructs the church as to the proper qualifications for eldership.

> **You younger men, likewise, be subject to your elders; and all of you, clothe yourselves with humility toward one another, for GOD IS OPPOSED TO THE PROUD, BUT GIVES GRACE TO THE HUMBLE.**
>
> **I Peter 5:5 NASB**

■   Peter instructs the young men of the church to submit to the church elders.

> **Obey your leaders, and submit to them; for they keep watch over your souls, as those who will give an account. Let them do this with joy and not with grief, for this would be unprofitable for you.**
>
> **Hebrews 13:17 NASB**

■   The writer of Hebrews instructs his readers to obey and submit to the elders.

> **For the overseer must be above reproach as God's steward, not self-willed, not quick-tempered, not addicted to wine, not pugnacious, not fond of sordid gain,**
>
> **holding fast the faithful word which is in accordance with the teaching, that he may be able**
>
> **both to exhort in sound doctrine and to refute those who contradict.**
>
> **Titus 1:7, 9 NASB**

> **But we request of you, brethren, that you appreciate those who diligently labor among you, and have charge over you in the Lord and give you instruction,**
>
> **I Thessalonians 5:12 NASB**

■   Paul teaches that elders are the household stewards, leaders, instructors and teachers of the local church.

How Eldership Teams Complement the Local Church

The structure of local church government makes a statement about the nature and philosophy of its ministry. The local church is not an undefined mass of people. It is a particular group of people and has a unique mission and purpose. The eldership government harmonizes and promotes the true nature of the local church. There are four obvious ways the eldership team complements the local church.

The Family Mentality of the Church

The Church is a family of brothers and sisters. The New Testament frequently used certain terms to describe the nature of the Church – the body, the bride and the flock. The most frequently used family term is the word "brethren." The reason behind this preference for the familial aspect of the Church is that only the most intimate of human relationships could express the love, closeness, privileges and relationship that exist between God and man, and man and man, as a result of Christ's incarnation and death. The local church is to be a close-knit family of brothers and sisters.

In complete obedience to the teachings of Christ, the early Christians and their leaders chose an appropriate leadership structure for their local congregation and that is leadership by a council of elders. They found within their biblical heritage a structure of government that was compatible with their new family and beliefs. Israel was a great family composed of many individual families. It found leadership by a plurality of elders to be a suitable form of self-government that provided fair representation for its members. The same is true of the local church today.

Non-Clerical Family

The second way the eldership complements the local church is that biblical eldership cannot exist in an environment of clericalism. The local church is a non-clerical family. The early Church was a people's movement. The distinguishing mark of Christianity was not found in a clerical hierarchy, but in the fact that God's Spirit came to dwell within ordinary, common people and that through them the Spirit manifested Jesus' life to the believing community and to the world.

Paul's employment of the eldership structure of government for the local church is clear, practical evidence against clericalism because the eldership is non-clerical in nature. The elders are always viewed in the Bible as "elders of the people," or "elders of the congregation," never "elders of God." The elders represent the people as leading members from among the people.

When establishing churches, Paul never ordained a priest or cleric to perform the church's ministry. When he established a church, he left behind a council of elders chosen from among the believers to jointly oversee the local community.

The Humble Servant Mentality of the Elders

The next way eldership complements the local church is they enhance the loving, humble servant character of the Christian family. The New Testament provides a consistent example of the eldership form of leadership as the ideal structure of leadership in a congregation where love, humility and servanthood are paramount. In order for an eldership team to operate effectively, the elders must show mutual regard for one another, submit themselves one to another, patiently wait upon one another, genuinely consider one another's interests and defer to one another. Eldership teams should enhance brotherly love, humility, mutuality, patience and loving interdependence. These are qualities that must be a mark of the local church.

Guarding and Promoting the Preeminence of Jesus Christ

Finally, eldership complements the local church by guarding and promoting the preeminence and position of Christ over the local church. Jesus left His disciples with the precious promise that "where two or three have gathered together in My name, there I am in their midst." Because the apostles knew that Jesus Christ by the Holy Spirit was uniquely present with them as Ruler, Head, Lord, Pastor, Master, Overseer, High Priest and King, they chose a form of government that reflected this truth. This concept was not a theoretical idea to the early Church. It was a reality.

CHAPTER III

THE BENEFITS OF PLURALITY
OF ELDERS

The underlying reason many Christians fear the plurality of elders is that they don't really understand the New Testament concept or its rich benefits to the local church. New Testament eldership is not, as many think, a high-status, board position that is open to any and all who desire membership. On the contrary, an eldership patterned on the New Testament model requires qualified elders who must meet specific moral and spiritual qualifications before they serve.

> **It is a trustworthy statement: if any man aspires to the office of overseer, it is a fine work he desires to do.**
>
> **An overseer, then, must be above reproach, the husband of one wife, temperate, prudent, respectable, hospitable, able to teach,**
>
> **not addicted to wine or pugnacious, but gentle, uncontentious, free from the love of money.**

He must be one who manages his own household well, keeping his children under control with all dignity

(but if a man does not know how to manage his own household, how will he take care of the church of God?);

and not a new convert, lest he become conceited and fall into the condemnation incurred by the devil.

And he must have a good reputation with those outside the church, so that he may not fall into reproach and the snare of the devil.

And let these also first be tested; then let them serve as deacons if they are beyond reproach.

I Timothy 3:1-7, 10 NASB

Do not lay hands upon anyone too hastily and thus share responsibility for the sins of others; keep yourself free from sin.

I Timothy 5:22 NASB

And when they had appointed elders for them in every church, having prayed with fasting, they commended them to the Lord in whom they had believed.

Acts 14:23 NASB

Such elders must be publicly examined by the Church as to their qualifications. They must be publicly installed into office. They must be motivated and empowered by the Holy Spirit to do their work. Finally, they must be acknowledged, loved and honored by the whole congregation. This honor given by the congregation includes the giving of financial support to elders who are uniquely gifted at preaching and teaching, which allows some elders to serve the church full or part time.

A Group of Equals

Leadership by a council of elders is a form of government found in nearly every society of the ancient Near East. It was the fundamental government structure of the nation of Israel throughout its Old Testament history. For Israel, a tribal society, the eldership was as basic as the family.

By definition, the eldership structure of government is a collective form of leadership in which each elder shares equally the position, authority and responsibility of the office. There are different names for this type of leadership structure. In contemporary terms, it is referred to as plurality or team leadership.

This great concept of a team of equals or a council of equals has enormous benefits. There are practical benefits that are provided to the local church family and its spiritual leaders as a result of the adoption of this concept.

Balancing Our Weaknesses

The first benefit is the bringing of balance to our weaknesses. We all have our blind spots and deficiencies. We can see these deficiencies clearly in others, but not in ourselves. Real wisdom is to realize that we sometimes have deficiencies and flaws that have hurt and frustrated others and, when nothing is done, will continue to hurt and frustrate people around you.

These deficiencies distort our judgment. They deceive us. They can even destroy us. This is very common among talented charismatic leaders. Because they are blinded to their own flaws and deficiencies, these leaders have destroyed themselves. They had no peers to confront and balance them. Some of them wanted none. For the individual on top of the structure of an organization, the essential balancing of one another's weaknesses is very important in order to have longevity of ministry and to build a healthy church.

Within a leadership team structure, its members complement and balance one another's weaknesses. If one of the elders has a tendency to act too harshly with people, the others can temper his harshness. Elders who are more doctrinally oriented can sharpen those who are more outreach oriented. Genuine single church pastors or set men would improve their character and ministries if they had genuine elders to whom they are regularly accountable and with whom they work jointly.

True Division of Labor

Two are better than one because they have a good return for their labor.

For if either of them falls, the one will lift up his companion. But woe to the one who falls when there is not another to lift him up.

Furthermore, if two lie down together they keep warm, but how can one be warm alone?

And if one can overpower him who is alone, two can resist him. A cord of three strands is not quickly torn apart.

Ecclesiastes 4:9-12 NASB

The second benefit is that it provides an atmosphere for true division of labor. The workload is lightened in a team leadership structure. Many pastors are ineffective because they suffer from severe battle fatigue. In an eldership team system of leadership, the heavy burdens are shared by a number of qualified functioning elders. King Solomon writes in Ecclesiastes "that two are better than one because they have a good return for their labor, for if either of them falls, the one will lift up his companion. But woe to the one who falls when there is not another to lift him up."

Specialized Gifting

The third benefit is that plurality of leadership allows each elder to function primarily according to personal gifting, rather than being forced to do everything and then being criticized for not being gifted enough. Every elder is forced to specialize in his particular gifting to help in the success of the local church. They have the opportunity to sharpen their gifting and calling, and willingly bring it to the table to add strength to where there is deficiency in the local assembly. There is no more pressure to be what you are not.

Accountability of Power

Fourth, an eldership team helps to provide a strong level of accountability. Power, it is said, tends to corrupt and absolute power corrupts absolutely. The plurality of leadership provides a formal structure for genuine accountability. Only when there is genuine accountability between equals in leadership is there any hope for breaking down the horrible abuse of pastoral authority that plagues many churches. Team leadership provides restraint on pride, greed and playing God. It serves as a check and balance on each other and as a safeguard against the very human tendency to play God over other people.

Accountability of Work

Finally, plurality of leadership by an eldership team provides the local church shepherd with accountability for his work. Church leaders sometimes can be lazy, forgetful, fearful or too busy to fulfill their responsibilities. They need people in ministry to whom they are answerable for their work. In the sports realm, athletes who train together push one another to greater achievement. When someone else is running alongside, a runner will push a little harder and go a little faster. The same is true in the kingdom of God. That is one reason the Lord sent His disciples out in twos.

The Set Man Among the Council of Equals

This is an extremely important principle that has been misunderstood. Simply because there is plurality of leadership does not mean that everyone is equal in gifting, in experience, in dedication, in biblical knowledge or in leadership ability. That is where the principle of the set man, or the first among equals, comes into play. Those among the elders who are particularly gifted leaders or teachers will naturally stand out among the other elders as leaders within a leadership body. The one who stands out because of genuine abilities and character ends up becoming the set man, the senior minister or the senior elder. This is what the Romans called *primus inter pares*, meaning "first among equals" or *primi inter pares* meaning "first ones among equals."

Jesus practiced this principle. He chose twelve apostles, all of whom He empowered to preach and heal, but He singled out three for special attention– Peter, James and John (first ones among equals). And then among the three, Peter stood out as the most prominent (first among equals).

> **And when He had come to the house, He did not allow anyone to enter with Him, except Peter and John and James, and the girl's father and mother.**
>
> **Luke 8:51 NASB**

> **And some eight days after these sayings, it came about that He took along Peter and John and James, and went up to the mountain to pray.**
>
> **Luke 9:28 NASB**

> **And He took with Him Peter and James and John, and began to be very distressed and troubled.**
>
> **Mark 14:33 NASB**

Among the twelve apostles, Peter, James, John and sometimes Andrew are "first ones among equals." On key occasions, Jesus chose only Peter, James and John to accompany Him to witness the power, glory and agony.

> **Now the names of the twelve apostles are these: The first, Simon, who is called Peter, and Andrew his brother; and James the son of Zebedee, and John his brother;**
>
> **Philip and Bartholomew; Thomas and Matthew the tax-gatherer; James the son of Alphaeus, and Thaddaeus;**
>
> **Simon the Zealot, and Judas Iscariot, the one who betrayed Him.**
>
> **Matthew 10:2-4 NASB**

And He appointed the twelve: Simon (to whom He gave the name Peter),

and James, the son of Zebedee, and John the brother of James (to them He gave the name Boanerges, which means, "Sons of Thunder");

and Andrew, and Philip, and Bartholomew, and Matthew, and Thomas, and James the son of Alphaeus, and Thaddaeus, and Simon the Zealot;

and Judas Iscariot, who also betrayed Him.

Mark 3:16-19 NASB

Simon, whom He also named Peter, and Andrew his brother; and James and John; and Philip and Bartholomew;

and Matthew and Thomas; James the son of Alphaeus, and Simon who was called the Zealot;

Judas the son of James, and Judas Iscariot, who became a traitor.

Luke 6:14-16 NASB

And when they had entered, they went up to the upper room, where they were staying; that is, Peter and John and James and Andrew, Philip and Thomas, Bartholomew and Matthew, James the son of Alphaeus, and Simon the Zealot, and Judas the son of James.

Acts 1:13 NASB

Among the three, as well as the twelve, Peter is unquestionably first among his equals. In all four lists of the apostles names, Peter's name is first. Matthew actually refers to Peter as "the first." By calling Peter "the first," Matthew means "first among his equals."

but I have prayed for you, that your faith may not fail; and you, when once you have turned again, strengthen your brothers."

Luke 22:32 NASB

Jesus charged Peter to "strengthen your brothers." Jesus acknowledged Peter as first among his brothers, the natural leader and motivator. He knew that they would need Peter's leadership to help them through the dark days immediately following their Lord's departure.

But on the contrary, seeing that I had been entrusted with the gospel to the uncircumcised, just as Peter had been to the circumcised

(for He who effectually worked for Peter in his apostleship to the circumcised effectually worked for me also to the Gentiles),

and recognizing the grace that had been given to me, James and Cephas and John, who were reputed to be pillars, gave to me and Barnabas the right hand of fellowship, that we might go to the Gentiles, and they to the circumcised.

Galatians 2:7-9 NASB

In Paul's letter to the Galatians, Paul speaks of James, Peter and John as the acknowledged "pastors" of the church in Jerusalem.

As the leader, the chief speaker, the man of action, Peter challenged, energized, strengthened and ignited the group. Without Peter, the group would have been less effective.

Please, we must understand that this does not mean, however, that elders who are first among their equals do all the thinking and decision-making for the group.

Pitfalls Set Men Must Avoid

There are dangers in every form of government or leadership structure administered by humans and the principle of "first among equals" is no exception.

First, there is the very real danger that the elders will relinquish their God-given responsibilities for the spiritual care of the church to one or two exceptionally gifted men. This danger will always exist because people are selfish and lazy by nature, particularly when it comes to spiritual matters. Once this happens, the elders are reduced to adviser status and the "first among equals" concept becomes "first without equals." Biblical eldership vanishes.

The second danger is that the set man principle in the concept of first among equals will be abused by a dominating, controlling leader. Such a leader may seek his own way and force out all dissent and disagreement.

Solutions

These dangers can be avoided if we attempt to do the following:

> **For the overseer must be above reproach as God's steward, not self-willed, not quick-tempered, not addicted to wine, not pugnacious, not fond of sordid gain,**
>
> **Titus 1:7 NASB**

> **shepherd the flock of God among you, exercising oversight not under compulsion, but voluntarily, according to the will of God; and not for sordid gain, but with eagerness;**
>
> **nor yet as lording it over those allotted to your charge, but proving to be examples to the flock.**

> **I Peter 5:2-3 NASB**

■ The local church and its leaders must be serious about the biblical requirements for elders. A "self-willed" man, a lording-it-over man, does not qualify to be a church leader according to the New Testament. Also, non-functioning elders, mere figureheads, are not qualified to serve as elders. If the local church is not solidly committed to having biblically qualified elders, it will find itself powerless to act against tyrants or idle leaders.

■ Elders need to work closely together as a united team, building trust and growing together. The elders meeting together is very important. It creates an opportunity to minister to one another, as well as doing business together. One of the secrets to a successful eldership is regular, effective meetings that include a major portion of time devoted to laboring together in prayer.

■ Elders need to be in the business of building up one another's lives. Older, more experienced elders need to mentor younger elders.

The Archenemy of Eldership

> **I know that after my departure savage wolves will come in among you, not sparing the flock;**

and from among your own selves men will arise,
speaking perverse things, to draw away the disciples
after them.

Therefore be on the alert, remembering that night
and day for a period of three years I did not cease to
admonish each one with tears.

Acts 20:29-31 NASB

The elders' archenemies are the false teachers. Paul
knew the enemy so well that he could say, "I know ... savage
wolves will come." There was no question about it. It was
going to happen. The wolves Paul speaks about are false
teachers who stalk the flock. They are called, "savage
wolves," a pack of large, fierce wolves who will not spare the
flock from destruction. They are strong and cunning. They
are persistent and come from every side. They are insatiable
and merciless in their appetite for devouring Christians. Their
presence can only bring death, confusion and destruction.

They eagerly seek you, not commendably, but they
wish to shut you out, in order that you may seek
them.

Galatians 4:17 NASB

Paul goes on to predict something even more subtle and
frightening than wolves. He warns that false teachers will
arise from within the congregation. Not only will wolves
come in to destroy the flock, men from within God's flock
professing to be Christians will emerge as false teachers.
Such men expose themselves by teaching "perverse things."
Paul means that they will teach perversions of God's holy
truth, twisted, distorted and heretical doctrine. They will not
outrightly deny the truth of God's Word, for that would be too
obvious and ineffective for Satan's purposes. Instead, they

will pervert truth. As masters of subtlety and novelty, they will mix truth with error, reinterpret truth, and change the meaning of words to give the illusion of truth. False teachers want followers, so they seek to draw away members of churches after them. They try to tear Christians away from the flock and its Spirit-placed leaders or overseers. They care nothing for the Church's unity and safety. They care only for themselves.

Solutions to False Teachers

Therefore be on the alert, remembering that night and day for a period of three years I did not cease to admonish each one with tears.

Acts 20:31 NASB

Paul's solution to the threat of false teachers is to be on the "alert." The word "alert" is from the Greek word *gregoreo* which literally means "keep awake" or "not sleep." It is most often used figuratively in the New Testament to mean "be wakeful," "be vigilant," "stay awake and ready for action." In this instance, it is a present tense imperative command that means "keep on being alert and ready for action." It implies a conscientious effort, a mental and spiritual attitude of alertness.

To strengthen and clarify his exhortation to be alert, Paul calls upon the elders to remember his example, "remembering that night and day for a period of three years, I did not cease to admonish each one with tears." What Paul is saying is that his own life is a study of pastoral vigilance in action. Paul's vigilant protection of the flock entailed a ministry of admonition which means "to warn," "to advise" or "to counsel." To admonish is to exert a corrective influence in a positive and caring way.

The reason for being alert is not just to be informed but to act. Both imperative commands, "be on guard" and "be on the alert" imply action. A good shepherd is never passive. He knows the necessity for acting quickly and decisively in the face of danger. He knows when he must fight and when he must stand his ground. To be aware of danger and not to act is to be a lazy, cowardly shepherd who betrays the flock. Elders must act because God has given them the authority to lead and protect the flock. They do not do this work on their own authority. The Holy Spirit placed them as overseers in the flock for the purpose of shepherding the Church. They have the authority to act as shepherds and overseers.

CHAPTER IV

SUBMISSION TO THE ELDERS OF THE LOCAL CHURCH

Remember those who led you, who spoke the word of God to you; and considering the result of their conduct, imitate their faith.

Obey your leaders, and submit to them; for they keep watch over your souls, as those who will give an account. Let them do this with joy and not with grief, for this would be unprofitable for you.

Hebrews 13:7, 17 NASB

It is tremendously important that Christians understand God's will regarding submission and obedience to their spiritual guides. More than any New Testament passage, Hebrews 13:17 addresses the believers duty to obey and submit to God ordained leadership. By using two very important verbs, "obey" and "submit," the Bible intensifies this exhortation. Although it is sometimes difficult to distinguish the precise differences in meaning between these two verbs, "submit" is the stronger and broader of the two.

Christians are not only to "obey" their leaders, meaning "to listen to" and "to follow," but are to "submit," meaning to "yield," "give way" and "defer" to them. This means that believers are to be responsive to their leaders, to yield to their authority and to subordinate themselves to them, even when they have a difference of opinion.

Obedience and submission to authority is fundamental to Christian living. Submission is the fruit of genuine humility and faith. It is the mark of the Spirit-filled life. True submission to God naturally expresses itself in obedience and submission to earthly authority, whether in the home, in marriage, at work, in society and in the local assembly of believers.

The effectiveness of any body of church leaders is measurably affected by the response of the people they lead. People who are stubborn and unsubmissive are unteachable and incapable of changing for their own good. Only when believers properly submit to their spiritual leaders does the local church have any chance to be the growing, loving, joyous family God intends it to be.

The Scriptures admonish that spiritual leaders be obeyed because "they keep watch over your souls." The verb "keep watch" literally means "keep oneself awake," but in the Scripture it is used metaphorically for watching, guarding or caring for people. Like the ancient city watchmen or shepherds of a flock, spiritual leaders must always be keenly alert, conscientious and diligent. Watchfulness demands tireless effort, self-discipline and selfless concern for the safety of others. These leaders are involved in spiritual care. They are keeping watch for "your souls." The Greek term for soul is *psyche*. In many instances, *psyche* is used as the equivalent of "person" or "oneself." We can then render *psyche* by the personal pronoun "you," which some translations do. However, in the context of this Scripture, *psyche* seems to have a deeper meaning that relates to the inward, spiritual dimension of life.

Keeping watch implies potential danger. Watching implies keeping oneself and others safe where danger is known to exist, or where one fears its existence. Where no danger exists, watching is not needed. Since false teachers and spiritual pitfalls abound, since all Christians start out as newborn babes in Christ, and since some Christians are perpetually weak in faith, watching over the spiritual development of God's people is indispensable.

> **When I say to the wicked, You shall surely die; and you do not warn him or speak out to warn the wicked from his wicked way that he may live, that wicked man shall die in his iniquity, but his blood I will require at your hand.**
>
> **Yet if you have warned the wicked, and he does not turn from his wickedness or from his wicked way, he shall die in his iniquity; but you have delivered yourself.**
>
> **Ezekiel 3:18-19 NASB**

Not only do spiritual leaders deserve to be obeyed because they keep watch for God's people, but their greater responsibility requires a stricter scrutiny and standard of accountability before God. All spiritual leaders are watchmen and shepherds "who will give an account." Jesus said that to whom much is given, much is required. Like the watchmen of a city, spiritual leaders are keenly aware that they will have to give an account to God for the critical task entrusted to them.

The Result of Submission

I have no greater joy than this, to hear of my children walking in the truth.

III John 4 NASB

The result of submission on the part of those who are led is deep, satisfying joy on the part of those who lead. Every leader knows the inexpressible joy of seeing lives transformed by the power of the gospel, watching people grow as a result of teaching the Word and seeing the flock prosper. John the apostle expressed this joy. What joy? The joy of seeing his children walking in the truth. This joy, which every leader has a right to expect, is possible only when the people obey and submit to their leader.

When God's people disobey, complain and fight against the leaders that God has placed over their lives, the joys of shepherding vanish. When Christians refuse to heed their leader's warning, the shepherd feels "grief." The word "grief" can also be rendered "groan," "sigh" or "moaning." Grief expresses a strong inward emotion, an emotion that words are unable to articulate. The word grief also expresses a deep sorrow and longing for better conditions.

I alone am not able to carry all this people, because it is too burdensome for me.

So if Thou art going to deal thus with me, please kill me at once, if I have found favor in Thy sight, and do not let me see my wretchedness.

Numbers 11:14-15 NASB

44

God-ordained leaders groan in sorrow over those who refuse to grow, learn, change or receive correction. Moses grieved many times because of the people's disobedience and stubbornness. On one occasion, the stubbornness of the people became so intolerable that he demanded to die. Rebellious behavior takes its toll on leaders. Sometimes good leaders give up because of the painful and deep bites of disobedient sheep.

> **For he who eats and drinks, eats and drinks judgment to himself, if he does not judge the body rightly.**
>
> **For this reason many among you are weak and sick, and a number sleep.**
>
> **But if we judged ourselves rightly, we should not be judged.**
>
> **But when we are judged, we are disciplined by the Lord in order that we may not be condemned along with the world.**
>
> **So then, my brethren, when you come together to eat, wait for one another.**
>
> **If anyone is hungry, let him eat at home, so that you may not come together for judgment. And the remaining matters I shall arrange when I come.**

I Corinthians 11:29-34 NASB

Disobedience has an even more serious impact on the believer. The Bible says, "this would be unprofitable for you." To cut oneself off from God's watchmen or to run away from a leader's care is dangerous. The enemy may delude the mind of the believer or a bitter spirit may set in, preventing all growth and maturity.

CHAPTER V

APOSTOLIC REQUIREMENT FOR SPĪRITUAL ELDERSHIP

An overseer, then, must be above reproach, the husband of one wife, temperate, prudent, respectable, hospitable, able to teach,

I Timothy 3:2a NASB

The most common mistake made by churches that are eager to implement eldership is to appoint biblically unqualified men. Letting unqualified, unprepared men assume leadership in the church is very dangerous to the destiny and health of the local church. It is a time proven formula for failure.

It is very important that the right kind of men serve as elders and deacons. The offices of God's church are not honorary positions bestowed on individuals or family members who have attended church faithfully or who are senior in years. Eldership is not a board position that is filled by good friends, rich donors, charismatic personalities or family members. The church offices of both elder and deacon are open to all who meet the apostolic, biblical requirements.

In dealing with the troubled church in Ephesus, Paul insisted that a properly constituted Christian church must have qualified, approved elders.

> **I am writing these things to you, hoping to come to you before long;**
>
> **but in case I am delayed, I write so that you may know how one ought to conduct himself in the household of God, which is the church of the living God, the pillar and support of the truth.**
>
> **I Timothy 3:14-15 NASB**
>
> **It is a trustworthy statement: if any man aspires to the office of overseer, it is a fine work he desires to do.**
>
> **An overseer, then, must be above reproach, the husband of one wife, temperate, prudent, respectable, hospitable, able to teach,**
>
> **not addicted to wine or pugnacious, but gentle, uncontentious, free from the love of money.**
>
> **He must be one who manages his own household well, keeping his children under control with all dignity**
>
> **(but if a man does not know how to manage his own household, how will he take care of the church of God?);**
>
> **and not a new convert, lest he become conceited and fall into the condemnation incurred by the devil.**

And he must have a good reputation with those outside the church, so that he may not fall into reproach and the snare of the devil.

I Timothy 3:1-7 NASB

When directing Titus in how to organize churches on the island of Crete, Paul reminds Titus to appoint only morally and spiritually qualified men to be elders. By stating elder qualifications in a letter, Paul establishes a public list to guide the local church in its choice of elders and to empower it to hold its elders accountable.

For this reason I left you in Crete, that you might set in order what remains, and appoint elders in every city as I directed you,

namely, if any man be above reproach, the husband of one wife, having children who believe, not accused of dissipation or rebellion.

For the overseer must be above reproach as God's steward, not self-willed, not quick-tempered, not addicted to wine, not pugnacious, not fond of sordid gain,

but hospitable, loving what is good, sensible, just, devout, self-controlled,

holding fast the faithful word which is in accordance with the teaching, that he may be able both to exhort in sound doctrine and to refute those who contradict.

Titus 1:5-9 NASB

When writing to the churches scattered throughout northwestern Asia Minor, Peter speaks of the kinds of men who should be elders to shepherd the flock "not under compulsion, but voluntarily, according to the will of God, and not for sordid gain, but with eagerness, nor yet as lording over those allotted to your charge, but proving to be examples to the flock."

> **shepherd the flock of God among you, exercising oversight not under compulsion, but voluntarily, according to the will of God; and not for sordid gain, but with eagerness;**
>
> **nor yet as lording it over those allotted to your charge, but proving to be examples to the flock.**

I Peter 5:2-3 NASB

The New Testament places greater emphasis on the qualifications for eldership than any other form of leadership post. There are three important reasons why God demands these qualifications of church leaders.

First, the Scripture says that an elder must be of irreproachable moral character and capable in the use of Scripture because he is "God's steward," that is, God's household manager. An elder is entrusted with God's dearest and most costly possessions, His children. He acts on behalf of God's interest. No earthly monarch would dare think of hiring an immoral or incapable person to manage his estate. Nor would parents think of entrusting their children or family finances to an untrustworthy or incompetent person.

As stewards of God's household, elders have access to people's homes and the most intimate details of their lives. They have access to the people who are most vulnerable to deception or abuse. Therefore, church elders must be men who are well-known by the community, have proven integrity and are doctrinally sound.

Second, local church elders are to be living examples for the people to follow. They are to model the character and conduct that God desires for all His children. Since God calls His people to "be blameless and innocent, children of God above reproach in the midst of a crooked and perverse generation," it is necessary that those who lead God's people model godly living.

> **And it will be, like people, like priest; So I will punish them for their ways, And repay them for their deeds.**
>
> **Hosea 4:9 NASB**

> **A pupil is not above his teacher; but everyone, after he has been fully trained, will be like his teacher.**
>
> **Luke 6:40 NASB**

Whatever the leaders are, the people become. Jesus said, "everyone after he has been fully trained, will be like his teacher." Biblical history demonstrates that people will seldom rise above the spiritual level of their leadership. Because people are like sheep, shepherd elders have an extraordinarily powerful impact on the behavior, attitudes and thinking of the people.

Model Lives

> **It is a trustworthy statement: if any man aspires to the office of overseer, it is a fine work he desires to do.**

> **An overseer, then, must be above reproach, the husband of one wife, temperate, prudent, respectable, hospitable, able to teach,**
>
> **I Timothy 3:1-2 NASB**

■   If the elders are not sensible, balanced and self-controlled, their judgment will be characterized by ugly extremes which will cause the people to be extreme and unbalanced.

> **holding fast the faithful word which is in accordance with the teaching, that he may be able both to exhort in sound doctrine and to refute those who contradict.**
>
> **Titus 1:9 NASB**

■   If the elders do not faithfully hold to the authority of the Word, the people will not hold to it.

> **not addicted to wine or pugnacious, but gentle, uncontentious, free from the love of money.**
>
> **I Timothy 3:3 NASB**

> **For the overseer must be above reproach as God's steward, not self-willed, not quick-tempered, not addicted to wine, not pugnacious, not fond of sordid gain,**
>
> **Titus 1:7 NASB**

■   If the elders have a contentious spirit, the people will inevitably become contentious.

> **An overseer, then, must be above reproach, the husband of one wife, temperate, prudent, respectable, hospitable, able to teach,**
>
> **I Timothy 3:2 NASB**

namely, if any man be above reproach, the husband of one wife, having children who believe, not accused of dissipation or rebellion.

Titus 1:6 NASB

■ If the elders are not faithful, one-woman husbands, they will subtly encourage others to be unfaithful.

Third, the biblical qualifications protect the church from incompetent or morally unfit leaders. Some people push themselves into positions of church leadership to satisfy their unholy egos. Others are sadly deceived about their own ability and character. These standards for elders are especially important when churches must deal with dominating and stubborn church leaders who are incapable of truly seeing their sins and yet must be discharged from office. The elder qualifications empower each congregation and its leaders with the right and the objective means to hold back or remove unfit men from leadership.

The Primary Qualifications of Elders

Elders must be qualified to lead God's people. These qualifications are not different from those of any clergy or anyone called in to some form of authority in the body. From the New Testament perspective, any man in the congregation who desires to lead God's people and who meets God's requirements for the office can be a leader.

God does not require you to be wealthy, have social status, be old in age, have advanced academic degrees or even great spiritual gifts. The body of Christ does the congregation and the work of God a great disservice when we add our own requirements to God's qualifications. Our man-made requirements end up excluding qualified and needed men from leadership.

Moral and Spiritual Character

The first and important qualification is that of being "above reproach." What the words "above reproach" mean is defined by the character qualities that follow the term. In both of Paul's lists of elders qualifications, the first specific character virtue itemized is "the husband of one wife." This means that an elder must be above reproach in his marital and sexual life.

One of satan's oldest, most effective strategies for destroying the people of God is to adulterate the marriages of those who lead God's people. Satan knows that if he can defile the shepherds' marriages, the sheep will follow. The specific marital and family qualifications God requires for elders are meant to protect the whole church. So the church must insist that its leaders meet these qualifications before serving and while serving. Among Christian leaders, adultery and other sexual sins are at epidemic levels.

The other character qualities stress the elder's integrity, self-control and spiritual maturity. Since the elders govern the church body, they must be self-controlled in the use of money, alcohol and in the exercise of their pastoral authority. Since they are to be models of Christian living, they must be spiritually devout, righteous, lovers of good men, hospitable and morally above reproach before the non-Christian community. In pastoral work, relationship skills are very important. Elders that lead must be gentle, stable, sound minded and uncontentious.

Angry, hot-headed men hurt people. An elder must not have a dictatorial spirit or be quick-tempered or self-willed. He must not be a new Christian. He must be a spiritually mature, humble, true and proven disciple of Jesus Christ.

Abilities

In the list of the qualifications of an elder, three important requirements address the elder's ability to perform the task. He must:

- be able to manage his household well.

- provide a model of Christian living for others to follow.

- be able to teach and defend the faith.

Able to Manage the Family Household Well

He must be one who manages his own household well, keeping his children under control with all dignity

(but if a man does not know how to manage his own household, how will he take care of the church of God?);

I Timothy 3:4-5 NASB

An elder must be able to manage his household well. The Puritans referred to the family household as the "little church." This principle is in keeping with the Scriptural reasoning that if a man cannot shepherd his family, he cannot shepherd the extended family of the church.

Managing the local church is more like managing a family than managing a business or state. An individual can be a very successful businessman and a brilliant office manager and yet be a terrible church elder or father.

> But I say to the unmarried and to widows that it is good for them if they remain even as I.
>
> But if they do not have self-control, let them marry; for it is better to marry than to burn.
>
> But to the married I give instructions, not I, but the Lord, that the wife should not leave her husband
>
> (but if she does leave, let her remain unmarried, or else be reconciled to her husband), and that the husband should not send his wife away.
>
> But to the rest I say, not the Lord, that if any brother has a wife who is an unbeliever, and she consents to live with him, let him not send her away.
>
> And a woman who has an unbelieving husband, and he consents to live with her, let her not send her husband away.
>
> For the unbelieving husband is sanctified through his wife, and the unbelieving wife is sanctified through her believing husband; for otherwise your children are unclean, but now they are holy.
>
> Yet if the unbelieving one leaves, let him leave; the brother or the sister is not under bondage in such cases, but God has called us to peace.
>
> For how do you know, O wife, whether you will save your husband? Or how do you know, O husband, whether you will save your wife?

Only, as the Lord has assigned to each one, as God has called each, in this manner let him walk. And thus I direct in all the churches.

Was any man called already circumcised? Let him not become uncircumcised. Has anyone been called in uncircumcision? Let him not be circumcised.

Circumcision is nothing, and uncircumcision is nothing, but what matters is the keeping of the commandments of God.

Let each man remain in that condition in which he was called.

Were you called while a slave? Do not worry about it; but if you are able also to become free, rather do that.

For he who was called in the Lord while a slave, is the Lord's freedman; likewise he who was called while free, is Christ's slave.

You were bought with a price; do not become slaves of men.

Brethren, let each man remain with God in that condition in which he was called.

Now concerning virgins I have no command of the Lord, but I give an opinion as one who by the mercy of the Lord is trustworthy.

I think then that this is good in view of the present distress, that it is good for a man to remain as he is.

Are you bound to a wife? Do not seek to be released. Are you released from a wife? Do not seek a wife.

But if you should marry, you have not sinned; and if a virgin should marry, she has not sinned. Yet

such will have trouble in this life, and I am trying to
spare you.

But this I say, brethren, the time has been
shortened, so that from now on those who have
wives should be as though they had none;

and those who weep, as though they did not weep;
and those who rejoice, as though they did not
rejoice; and those who buy, as though they did not
possess;

and those who use the world, as though they did not
make full use of it; for the form of this world is
passing away.

But I want you to be free from concern. One who is
unmarried is concerned about the things of the
Lord, how he may please the Lord;

but one who is married is concerned about the
things of the world, how he may please his wife,

and his interests are divided. And the woman who is
unmarried, and the virgin, is concerned about the
things of the Lord, that she may be holy both in
body and spirit; but one who is married is
concerned about the things of the world, how she
may please her husband.

And this I say for your own benefit; not to put a
restraint upon you, but to promote what is seemly,
and to secure undistracted devotion to the Lord.

I Corinthians 7:8-35 NASB

What about single men and women? Or married men
and women who have no children? Can they be elders? Most
definitely. Single men and childless, married men can
certainly be elders. Where they lack experience because of
their unmarried or childless status, their fellow elders who are

married and have children can fill in the gap. The sexual conduct and home management of single and childless men must be above reproach, just as it must be above reproach for married men who have children.

Able to Provide a Model for Others to Follow

nor yet as lording it over those allotted to your charge, but proving to be examples to the flock.

I Peter 5:3 NASB

Be imitators of me, just as I also am of Christ.

I Corinthians 11:1 NASB

Brethren, join in following my example, and observe those who walk according to the pattern you have in us.

Philippians 3:17 NASB

An elder must be an example of Christian living that others will want to follow. If a man is not a godly model for others to follow, he cannot be an elder even if he is a good teacher and manager. The greatest way to inspire and influence people for God is through personal examples. Character and deeds are what really influence people. Oswald Sanders said in his book on spiritual leadership "that the final estimate of men shows that history cares not an iota for the rank or title a man has borne, or the office he has held, but only the quality of his deeds and the character of his mind and heart."

Able to Teach and Defend the Faith

An overseer, then, must be above reproach, the husband of one wife, temperate, prudent, respectable, hospitable, able to teach,

I Timothy 3:2 NASB

holding fast the faithful word which is in accordance with the teaching, that he may be able both to exhort in sound doctrine and to refute those who contradict.

Titus 1:9 NASB

An elder must be able to teach and defend the faith. It does not matter how successful a man is and how intelligent he is. If he is not firmly committed to apostolic doctrine and able to instruct people in biblical doctrine, he does not qualify as a biblical elder. The New Testament requires that an elder hold fast the faithful word which is in accordance with the teaching. This means that an elder must firmly adhere to historical and biblical teachings. Elders must not be chosen from among those who have been toying with new doctrines.

Since the local church is the pillar and support of the truth, its leaders must be solid on biblical doctrine or the church would crumble. The local church is like a group of flocks traveling over wolf-infested territories and, because of this, only leaders who know the way and see the wolves can lead the flock to its safe destination. An elder must be characterized by doctrinal integrity. An elder must be firmly committed to apostolic and biblical doctrine so that he may be able to exhort in sound doctrine and to refute those who contradict.

This means that a prospective elder has applied himself for some years to the reading and study of Scripture, that he can reason intelligently and logically discuss biblical issues, that he has formulated doctrinal beliefs, and that he has the verbal ability and willingness to teach others. He must be able to teach and exhort the congregation in sound doctrine and to defend the truth from false teachers.

CHAPTER VI

PROTECTING AN ELDER

Do not receive an accusation against an elder except on the basis of two or three witnesses.

I Timothy 5:19 NASB

A single witness shall not rise up against a man on account of any iniquity or any sin which he has committed; on the evidence of two or three witnesses a matter shall be confirmed.

Deuteronomy 19:15 NASB

Honoring an elder involves protecting him from malicious people and false accusations. We must not be naive about the fact that there are plenty of hateful, unstable people who aim to ruin people in authority. Godly men in the Bible like Joseph, Moses, David, Jeremiah, Nehemiah and Paul all experienced the bitter sting of false accusation. David, for example, pleaded with king Saul not to listen to false reports about his intentions toward him. In I Samuel 24:9, David said to Saul, "Why do you listen to the words of men, saying, Behold David seeks to harm?"

They hate him who reproves in the gate, And they abhor him who speaks with integrity.

Amos 5:10 NASB

Amos, the Old Testament farmer turned prophet, wrote "they hate him who reproves in the gate, and they abhor him who speaks with integrity." The more diligently and conscientiously an elder or a leader becomes involved in other's problems, the greater the risk of facing angry false accusations. When people become angry at their leaders, they think they have the right to strike out at them and say whatever they want to say. Scripture provides protection for elders by stating, "do not receive an accusation against an elder except on the basis of two or three witnesses." This means that you must not listen to unsubstantiated charges and don't automatically accept as true an accusation made against an elder.

The words of a whisperer are like dainty morsels, And they go down into the innermost parts of the body.

Proverbs 18:8 NASB

At heart we all love to hear rumors and scandals. But Christians are to be people of truth, love and light. Therefore, we must hate scandalous tales and unsupported rumors. We must silence them whenever we hear them because they are destructive and harmful to individual people and to the life of the community of the church. Good people have been ruined by unfounded accusations and we should do everything possible to avoid accusations.

He who covers a transgression seeks love, But he who repeats a matter separates intimate friends.

Proverb 17:9 NASB

Love always tries to see others in the best possible light and not the worst. Our judgments are to be governed by facts, evidence and witnesses, not rumors. We must live by the principle, "no judgment without the facts." We should not believe any story, even from our most trusted friends, until we have all the facts from the people involved.

We must understand that fair, reasonable protection from accusation does not imply immunity. Paul's statement is "except on the basis" or "on the evidence of two or three witnesses." This means that an accusation brought by two or three people who have witnessed the sin, or two or three people who have verified another's accusation, must be investigated and judged. An accusation of sin that is substantiated by witnesses must be heard. It cannot be brushed aside. As unpleasant and time consuming as a fair investigation into an accusation might be, it must be done.

CHAPTER VII

DISCIPLINING AN ELDER

Those who continue in sin, rebuke in the presence of all, so that the rest also may be fearful of sinning.

I Timothy 5:20 NASB

The Bible tells us how an elder should be treated if an accusation of sin is found to be true. An elder who has been proven to be guilty of sin by witnesses is to be rebuked before the church. The imperative verb "rebuke" translates the Greek word *elencho* which is a term conveying the ideas of "exposing," "proving guilt," "correcting" and "reproving." In this context, "rebuke" includes the ideas of public exposure, correction and reproof.

The context of this Scripture indicates that the sin to which Paul refers is very serious. It is "sin" and not merely a leadership blunder or minor shortcoming. Witnesses are required to verify the truth of the charges and a public rebuke is demanded which would not be required of minor offenses. Godly wisdom, counsel and prayer are the only things that will guide the local church and its spiritual leaders in implementing these instructions in individual cases.

so that the rest also may be fearful of sinning.

I Timothy 5:20b NASB

A spiritual leader's sin must be treated with great concern because it has grave ramifications. It can lead more people astray and can cause the unbelieving world to mock God. If the world sees that local churches take sin seriously, especially in the discipline of sinning leaders, then it will believe that Christians mean what they preach. Also, only when the discipline of an erring church leader is made public is there any chance of controlling one of the most divisive forces in a church and that is rumor-mongering, gossip and misinformation.

Public rebuke of an elder who sins fulfills another important purpose: "that the rest also may be fearful of sinning." Not only the public discipline for the correction of the sinning elder, it is also for deterring others from sin. "The rest" seems to refer not only to the other elders, but so the entire congregation would also experience some measure of fear. The phrase, "of sinning," is not in the original text which reads, "so that the rest also may have fear." The fear the elder would experience includes not only the fear of sinning, but the shame of public exposure. To see the sin of a fellow elder publicly exposed before the church would produce a fear of sinning and of its shameful consequences. God uses such fear as a powerful deterrent to keep people, especially church leaders, from sinning.

CHAPTER VIII

HONORING ELDERS

Let the elders who rule well be considered worthy of double honor, especially those who work hard at preaching and teaching.

For the Scripture says, YOU SHALL NOT MUZZLE THE OX WHILE HE IS THRESHING, and The laborer is worthy of his wages.

Do not receive an accusation against an elder except on the basis of two or three witnesses.

Those who continue in sin, rebuke in the presence of all, so that the rest also may be fearful of sinning.

I solemnly charge you in the presence of God and of Christ Jesus and of His chosen angels, to maintain these principles without bias, doing nothing in a spirit of partiality.

Do not lay hands upon anyone too hastily and thus share responsibility for the sins of others; keep yourself free from sin.

No longer drink water exclusively, but use a little wine for the sake of your stomach and your frequent ailments.

The sins of some men are quite evident, going before them to judgment; for others, their sins follow after.

Likewise also, deeds that are good are quite evident, and those which are otherwise cannot be concealed.

I Timothy 5:17-25 NASB

In verses 17 and 18, Paul admonishes the congregation to care for the welfare of elders who rule well, particularly those who labor at preaching and teaching the Word. The elders that the apostle Paul is referring to here are identified by two qualifying clauses "who rule well" and "those who work hard at preaching and teaching the word." Elders who lead well deserve "double honor," but "above all," those who work hard at preaching and teaching.

Although all elders rule, certain elders deserve double honor or financial support because they "rule well." The word "rule" is the Greek word *prohistemi*, which means to "lead," to "care for," to "manage" and "to direct." The idea is that these elders exercise effective pastoral leadership. These kinds of elders talked about here are natural leaders, visionaries, planner, organizers and motivators. These are the kind of men who get things done and can effectively care for people. Moreover, they are willing and able to give a good deal of their time, skill and energy to the spiritual care of the local congregation. In addition, these elders "work hard" at preaching and teaching. Because these elders diligently lead and teach the congregation, Paul exhorts, "let them be considered worthy," which means "rightfully deserving" or "entitled to." Because of their skills and strenuous labor, such elders are rightfully entitled to double honor.

Elders who teach and preach, "work hard" at long hours of study, preparation, prayer and demanding teaching situations. Preaching and teaching is absorbing work. It is mentally strenuous, time-consuming work that demands a great deal of strength and self-discipline. It has been estimated that a half-hour of preaching and teaching can use as much physical energy as eight hours of manual labor.

Laboring Elders Versus Non-laboring Elders

Let the elders who rule well be considered worthy of double honor, especially those who work hard at preaching and teaching.

For the Scripture says, YOU SHALL NOT MUZZLE THE OX WHILE HE IS THRESHING, and The laborer is worthy of his wages.

I Timothy 5:17-18 NASB

The question that comes to mind is: who are these kinds of elders that the Bible says labor at teaching, since all elders are required to be "able to teach?" What is the difference between these elders? The answer is actually found in the phrase "who labor" or "those that work hard." Not all elders of a local congregation or church "labor hard" or "work hard." Some labor more than others.

The reason these elders work hard or labor over the Word and doctrine is because they are spiritually gifted to do so. They are driven to study Scripture and to work fully at teaching. Nothing else satisfies them like teaching and preaching God's Word. They are skilled at communicating divine truth and there is a marked effectiveness to their teaching. The people that they teach have confidence that they are knowledgeable in doctrine. Their teaching bears consistent fruit. Although all elders must be able to teach, not all elders are Spirit gifted teachers and shepherds who labor in the Word.

Differences in spiritual giftedness must not be allowed to create jealousy or division within the eldership. By stating God's approval of such elders and their entitlement to double honor, Paul emphasizes that these elders ought to be viewed by the congregation and their fellow elders as a source of blessing, joy and profit, rather than as a threat.

It is also very important to understand that just because the teaching and shepherding gifts are important to a local church, the New Testament does not elevate those who possess these gifts to special status, nor does it create a distinct office separate from the eldership team.

How Double Honor Is Given to an Elder

All elders should be honored, but elders who rule well and work hard at preaching and teaching are entitled to "double honor." By using the expression "double honor," Paul wisely avoids slighting other elders of their due honor and is able to call special attention to those who rule well and those who labor at teaching. Double honor refers to honor for an elder of the church and honor for his extra labor.

For the Scripture says, YOU SHALL NOT MUZZLE THE OX WHILE HE IS THRESHING, and The laborer is worthy of his wages.

I Timothy 5:18 NASB

The word honor means "respect," "consideration," or "high regard" and in certain instances includes the idea of monetary aid. Paul feels very strongly about the congregation's duty to care for elders who labor in the Word. He wants no misunderstanding as to the meaning or necessity of his instruction, so in verse 18 he adds scriptural support and clarification to his charge. Quoting from both the Old and New Testaments, Paul says, "for the scripture says you shall not muzzle the ox while he is threshing, and the laborer is worthy of his wages." By using this qualifying phrase, Paul is saying that complete unity exists between the Old and New Testaments. Both Moses and Jesus agree that a laboring man is "worthy of his wages."

You shall not muzzle the ox while he is threshing.

Deuteronomy 25:4 NASB

Paul's Old Testament quotation is from the above Scripture which says, "you shall not muzzle the ox while he is threshing." The context of Deuteronomy concerns equity and justice in daily life, even the right of an animal to enjoy the fruit of its labor while working for its owner.

For it is written in the Law of Moses, YOU SHALL NOT MUZZLE THE OX WHILE HE IS THRESHING. God is not concerned about oxen, is He?

I Corinthians 9:9 NASB

For the Scripture says, YOU SHALL NOT MUZZLE THE OX WHILE HE IS THRESHING, and The laborer is worthy of his wages.

I Timothy 5:18 NASB

Twice in the New Testament is Deuteronomy 25:4 quoted to support the right of men of God to receive material sustenance for their labors. To refuse to support hard-working elders or leaders of the Word is as unjust, heartless and selfish as muzzling an animal while it is working, which was a common practice among greedy ancient farmers. Paul's New Testament quotation, "the laborer is worthy of his wages" is from Luke 10:7. Jesus originally spoke these words to the seventy before He sent them out to preach. No matter how poor a local congregation is, it must exercise faith and liberality before the Lord in giving to those who labor in the Word. God's people must learn to honor their elders.

The Elder's Rights

Do I not have as much freedom as anyone else? Am I not an apostle? Haven't I seen Jesus our Lord with my own eyes? Isn't it because of my hard work that you are in the Lord?

Even if others think I am not an apostle, I certainly am to you, for you are living proof that I am the Lord's apostle.

This is my answer to those who question my authority as an apostle.

Don't we have the right to live in your homes and share your meals?

Don't we have the right to bring a Christian wife along with us as the other disciples and the Lord's brothers and Peter do?

Or is it only Barnabas and I who have to work to support ourselves?

What soldier has to pay his own expenses? And have you ever heard of a farmer who harvests his crop and doesn't have the right to eat some of it? What shepherd takes care of a flock of sheep and isn't allowed to drink some of the milk?

And this isn't merely human opinion. Doesn't God's law say the same thing?

For the law of Moses says, "Do not keep an ox from eating as it treads out the grain." Do you suppose God was thinking only about oxen when he said this?

Wasn't he also speaking to us? Of course he was. Just as farm workers who plow fields and thresh the grain expect a share of the harvest, Christian workers should be paid by those they serve.

I Corinthians 9:1-10 NLT

In the day of the great Apostle Paul, there were sceptics in Corinth that questioned Paul's authority and rights as an apostle. In verse one of the above, we see Paul giving his credentials — he actually had a personal encounter with the Lord Jesus Christ. He had seen and talked with the resurrected Christ Who called him to be who he was, an apostle (see Acts 9:3-18). In that case, his known credentials make his letter to the Corinthians more persuasive.

As in any ministry, the fruits that are borne are the evidence of God's approval. The lives that were being changed were evidence to the people that God was in fact using Paul. In verse four, Paul begins to explain his rights as an apostle, as a leader, as a Christian worker. Paul uses himself as an illustration of the rights to have hospitality, to be married and to be paid for his work. However, we find out that Paul waived these rights for good reasons.

> When you enter a town, don't move around from home to home. Stay in one place, eating and drinking what they provide you. Don't hesitate to accept hospitality, because those who work deserve their pay.

> **Luke 10:7 NLT**

Jesus said here that workers deserve their wages. Paul above echoed Jesus' principle and urged the church to be sure to properly compensate their Christian workers. We have the awesome responsibility to care for our pastors, teachers, missionaries and other spiritual leaders. It is our duty and privilege to see that those who serve us in the ministry are fairly and adequately compensated.

> We have planted good spiritual seed among you. Is it too much to ask, in return, for mere food and clothing?

> If you support others who preach to you, shouldn't we have an even greater right to be supported? Yet we have never used this right. We would rather put up with anything than put an obstacle in the way of the Good News about Christ.

> Don't you know that those who work in the Temple get their meals from the food brought to the Temple as offerings? And those who serve at the altar get a share of the sacrificial offerings.

> In the same way, the Lord gave orders that those who preach the Good News should be supported by those who benefit from it.

> Yet I have never used any of these rights. And I am not writing this to suggest that I would like to start now. In fact, I would rather die than lose my distinction of preaching without charge.

> For preaching the Good News is not something I can boast about. I am compelled by God to do it. How terrible for me if I didn't do it!

If I were doing this of my own free will, then I would deserve payment. But God has chosen me and given me this sacred trust, and I have no choice.

What then is my pay? It is the satisfaction I get from preaching the Good News without expense to anyone, never demanding my rights as a preacher.

This means I am not bound to obey people just because they pay me, yet I have become a servant of everyone so that I can bring them to Christ.

I Corinthians 9:11-19 NLT

Paul goes on to further clarify the rights of a leader. In verse twelve, Paul says, "We have never used this right." In other words, Paul had consciously not looked for assistance when doing ministry in Corinth. Why? First of all, Paul could have asked the Corinthian church for financial support, especially since Jesus Himself had endorsed that people of ministry should be supported by those who benefit from their ministry (Matthew 10:10). But Paul was concerned with being misunderstood and misinterpreted.

You see, we are not like those hucksters--and there are many of them--who preach just to make money. We preach God's message with sincerity and with Christ's authority. And we know that the God who sent us is watching us.

II Corinthians 2:17 NLT

At that time, Corinth was infested with false teachers who hoped to make a good profit from preaching. And as a matter of fact, Paul was being cautious not to look like one of them. So he completely separated himself from those false teachers in order to silence the critics of that day who said he was only doing God's work for money. Paul willingly surrendered his rights in order to win people to Christ. Often, when your focus is on living for Christ, your rights become unimportant in comparison.

It is worth noting that Paul even questioned his choice afterward. He stated that, "I robbed other churches by accepting their contributions so I could serve you at no cost." Perhaps Paul felt this way because the Corinthians might have thought that preachers could be judged by how much money they demanded. A good speaker demanded the most. An average speaker would be a little cheaper and a poor speaker would speak for free. As a weapon against God's man Paul, the false teachers may have argued that Paul was a rookie because he gave "freebies." This practice is still in operation today. But we must be very careful because those eloquent teachers and preachers who man the pulpits of today and who charge enormous honorariums might have to take a back seat to those God is raising up who have yet to receive a seed for their work. Beware of this!

Eating While Working

And this isn't merely human opinion. Doesn't God's law say the same thing?

For the law of Moses says, "Do not keep an ox from eating as it treads out the grain." Do you suppose God was thinking only about oxen when he said this?

Wasn't he also speaking to us? Of course he was. Just as farm workers who plow fields and thresh the grain expect a share of the harvest, Christian workers should be paid by those they serve.

I Corinthians 9:8-10 NLT

Paul uses part of this Scripture to quote the saying again from Deuteronomy 25:4. Oxen in the Old Testament were often used to tread out the grain on a threshing floor. The animal was fastened by poles to a large millstone. As it walked around an area 100-feet in diameter, it would trample the grain with its hoofs, separating the kernels from the chaff. At the same time, the millstone ground the grain into flour. To muzzle the ox or to tie its mouth would prevent it from eating while it was working. This would weaken the beast as well as cheat it. Paul uses this illustration in the New Testament to argue that people who are productive in Christian work, especially pastors and other leaders, should not be denied its benefits — financial support — or unfairly paid.

Work Done Well Is Work Paid Well

Elders who do their work well should be paid well, especially those who work hard at both preaching and teaching.

For the Scripture says, "Do not keep an ox from eating as it treads out the grain." And in another place, "Those who work deserve their pay!"

I Timothy 5:17-18 NLT

Faithful church leaders should be supported and appreciated. Too often and too commonly, leaders are the targets of criticism because their congregational members hold such unrealistic expectations of them. Let me ask you this: How do you treat your church leaders? Do you enjoy finding fault? Or do you take pleasure in displaying your appreciation? Have you spoken a word of encouragement to them lately? Ask yourself: At your church, do your pastors and other leaders receive enough financial support to allow them to live without worrying about their needs or their families? Jesus and Paul consistently emphasized the importance of supporting and appreciating those who lead and teach us.

A Little Respect

Dear brothers and sisters, honor those who are your leaders in the Lord's work. They work hard among you and warn you against all that is wrong.

I Thessalonians 5:12 NLT

The quote here, "Those who are your leaders in the Lord's work" speaks of the pastors and the elders of the local church. The question should arise: How can you show respect to your pastor and other church leaders? You must express your appreciation. Tell them how you have been helped or imparted by their leadership, teachings or lifestyle, and then thank them openly. If you remain silent, how will they really know where you stand with them? All leaders need and deserve your support and love. All shepherds love to be blessed by their sheep. It is an incredible experience.

The Response of a Student

Those who are taught the word of God should help their teachers by paying them.

Galatians 6:6 NLT

In the secular world, there is a saying: "An apple a day keeps the doctor away" and because of this many secular teachers are given bright, shiny red apples in grade school. This is the student's response of admiration and care for their teacher or instructor.

Thank God for apples today, but apples couldn't save us in the Garden and they can't save us today. We need money to live. Paul was not shy in relating this. He said that students of the Word should take care of their teachers. In the Scripture, Paul cuts to the chase and says, "Students help your teachers by paying them." It is easy to receive good Bible teachings and then turn around and take our spiritual leaders for granted, ignoring their financial and physical needs.

We should care for those who teach us Biblical truths. And this should be done, not grudgingly or reluctantly, but with a generous spirit, showing honor and appreciation for all they have done.

Let him that is taught in the word communicate unto him that teacheth in all good things.

Galatians 6:6 KJV

The King James Version of this Scripture uses an interesting word "communicate." The original Greek word for communicate is the word *koinoneo*, a form of the word *koinonia* which means, "communion and fellowship." This word communicates means to share with others, to distribute, to be partakers or to partnership with. In other words, the Scripture tells us that we who are taught (through the teaching and preaching of the Good News) should communicate (share with, distribute to, be a partaker with and partnership with) him who teaches and preaches the Good News (the good thing!). And what better way today to do this than by blessing our pastor or other leaders that work in the Word with financial support.

How to Receive a Well-Earned Reward

How grateful I am, and how I praise the Lord that you are concerned about me again. I know you have always been concerned for me, but for a while you didn't have the chance to help me.

Not that I was ever in need, for I have learned how to get along happily whether I have much or little.

I know how to live on almost nothing or with everything. I have learned the secret of living in every situation, whether it is with a full stomach or empty, with plenty or little.

For I can do everything with the help of Christ who gives me the strength I need.

But even so, you have done well to share with me in my present difficulty.

As you know, you Philippians were the only ones who gave me financial help when I brought you the Good News and then traveled on from Macedonia. No other church did this.

Even when I was in Thessalonica you sent help more than once.

I don't say this because I want a gift from you. What I want is for you to receive a well-earned reward because of your kindness.

At the moment I have all I need--more than I need! I am generously supplied with the gifts you sent me with Epaphroditus. They are a sweet-smelling sacrifice that is acceptable to God and pleases him.

And this same God who takes care of me will supply all your needs from his glorious riches, which have been given to us in Christ Jesus.

Now glory be to God our Father forever and ever. Amen.

Philippians 4:10-20 NLT

I believe it is very significant that Paul penned this particular portion of Scripture which captures his gratitude toward the Philippians for walking in the principle of support for a "worker for Christ." We also get a chance to see the reward. The imbalance of those walking in the principle versus not walking in it.

First, Paul comments that he is grateful to the Philippian church for showing concern for him. How did they show concern for him? They supported him. They sent financial support to Paul to help pay the expenses he incurred while doing the work of the ministry.

> I know how to live on almost nothing or with everything. I have learned the secret of living in every situation, whether it is with a full stomach or empty, with plenty or little.
>
> For I can do everything with the help of Christ who gives me the strength I need.
>
> But even so, you have done well to share with me in my present difficulty.

Philippians 4:12-14 NLT

Paul tells the Philippian church that no matter what circumstances and situations he faced, Christ always had his back. The strength of Christ is what allowed him to stay afloat, no matter how hard his living situation was. But Paul was very grateful to receive support at this time because he was facing some current difficulties.

> As you know, you Philippians were the only ones who gave
> me financial help when I brought you the Good News and
> then traveled on from Macedonia. No other church did
> this.
>
> Even when I was in Thessalonica you sent help more than
> once.

> ### Philippians 4:15-16 NLT

We find here that during Paul's missionary journeys, it
was the Philippian church that solely cared for him. This was
the only church that "communicated" with him. They became
partakers of his ministry. The Philippians became Paul's
partners in the ministry. The Bible says that even when Paul
was not around, and was ministering in Thessalonica, the
Philippian believers were still sending seeds. Why? Because
they understood the principle that every Christian laborer is
worthy of his hire. They understood the principle of seed
time and harvest.

> I don't say this because I want a gift from you. What I want
> is for you to receive a well-earned reward because of your
> kindness.

> ### Philippians 4:17 NLT

> Not because I desire a gift: but I desire fruit that may
> abound to your account.

> ### Philippians 4:17 KJV

Paul tells the Philippian church that he commends them
for their gracious act. The Philippians shared in Paul's
financial support while he was in prison. When we give to
those in need, it not only blesses the receiver, it benefits the
giver as well. Paul tells them that his words of
encouragement and thanksgiving were not because he wanted

gifts, but Paul said he was looking for them to "receive a well-earned reward." The King James Version says that he desired, "fruit that may abound to your account." We all have heavenly accounts that earn (and lose) "rewards." We earn these rewards from righteous acts done here on earth. It was not the Philippians' gift, but their spirit of love and devotion that Paul appreciated most.

Like the Philippian church of their time, very few believers are consistently supporting their pastors or leaders as they fulfill their duties in ministry. Because of this, many of God's leaders are forced to take secular jobs which drain them of their time and energy to balance the responsibilities of life, the family and their personal obligations. Other leaders find it necessary to go on the road to minister in other churches to receive honorariums to "live." This becomes dangerous because the motive behind it often gets cloudy and, before you know it, many good anointed leaders gradually have been transformed into hirelings. Once traveling to minister the Gospel becomes the solution in your mind to pay your bills at home, you have allowed the waters of your calling to become muddy. This is very dangerous, and yet it happens so frequently. Local houses are not shouldering their responsibility, and so they force their man of God to become a "road runner." Sad to say, many "road runners" have been bitten by the "coyote" of their lives and have become hirelings.

The Right to Honor

As it happened, Publius's father was ill with fever and dysentery. Paul went in and prayed for him, and laying his hands on him, he healed him.

Then all the other sick people on the island came and were cured.

As a result we were showered with honors, and when the time came to sail, people put on board all sorts of things we would need for the trip.

Acts 28:8-10 NLT

We have seen that it is the right of the pastor, and any of the leaders that teach God's Word, to be supported by those who are benefitting, those whose lives are changed. The pastor is worthy of double honor (1 Timothy 5:17-18). We must begin to properly honor those that labor among us. In the Scripture above Paul was found doing ministry work. But the Bible records that the recipients showed respect by honoring him after the great, righteous deeds were done. They blessed him as they sent him off to do more great deeds.

Do you support your pastor? Are others in your local church "communicating" to the pastor and the other church leaders there? Are you sowing into other ministries and ignoring the gift in front of you? If the announcement was made at church this Sunday that everyone is to come and support their pastor financially, would you become upset? Guess what? It is the elder's right.

CHAPTER IX

ESTEEMING THE LEADERS OVER YOU

> **But we request of you, brethren, that you
> appreciate those who diligently labor among you,
> and have charge over you in the Lord and give
> you instruction,**
>
> **and that you esteem them very highly in love
> because of their work. Live in peace with one
> another.**

I Thessalonians 5:12-13 NASB

Although the church in Thessalonica was but a few months old (one to three months) and lacked its founding fathers because of the fierce hostility to the gospel there, Paul exhorts the infant congregation to recognize and love the leaders over them. To better appreciate Paul's exhortation to the Thessalonians to acknowledge church leaders, we must remember that there were at that time no distinctions between clergy and laity. There was no officialism and there were no priestly garments to distinguish certain members. Those who deserve recognition are first described as "those who diligently labor among you." The word labor is a term used to describe manual labor.

It is a strong word denoting toil and strenuous work that results in weakness and fatigue. It is a favorite Pauline word. The phrase "diligently labor" reveals an important aspect of eldership, which is hard work. Caring for people's spiritual welfare is stressful work. It is emotionally draining, time consuming and often monotonous and discouraging. It requires a great deal of personal dedication and sacrifice. The phrase "among you" shows that the labor is on behalf of the local congregation and not labor for personal employment. Biblical eldership is not a church board that conducts business for two or three hours a month. It is a hard working pastoral body. Paul appeals to the Thessalonian congregation to acknowledge all those who lead and admonish them. In verse 13 he appeals to the congregation to "esteem them very highly in love."

Superabundantly

Render to all what is due them: tax to whom tax is due; custom to whom custom; fear to whom fear; honor to whom honor.

Romans 13:7 NASB

Honor all men; love the brotherhood, fear God, honor the king.

I Peter 2:17 NASB

**And Paul said, I was not aware, brethren, that he
was high priest; for it is written, YOU SHALL NOT
SPEAK EVIL OF A RULER OF YOUR PEOPLE.**

Acts 23:5 NASB

The magnitude to which the church is to esteem its
leaders is expressed by the intensive adverb "very highly"
which means "superabundantly" or "most exceedingly." God
cares about how people treat those who are in authority. The
Bible exhorts us not only to obey but to honor our rulers.
When Paul, for example, realized he had spoken rudely to the
high priest Ananias, he apologized by saying, "I was not
aware, brethren, that he was high priest, for it is written: you
shall not speak evil of a ruler of your people." If the
disobedience and ingratitude of people toward their civil
leaders concerns God deeply, imagine how much greater is
His concern that His people properly honor their spiritual
leaders. Our natural tendency is to take our leaders for
granted, forget what they have done for us, complain rather
than be thankful, accentuate the bad and disregard the good.
God gave Israel some of the greatest leaders in human history.
Yet during difficult times, the people were ready in a moment
to stone both Moses and David.

Loving Your Man of God

In addition to, "esteem them very highly," Paul adds the
beautiful and comprehensive phrase "in love." We usually
emphasize the importance of church shepherds loving the
people and that is important, but here Paul turns the tables and
charges the people to love their shepherds or their leaders. To
Paul, love is the divine glue that holds the leaders and
congregation together through all the disagreements and hurts
of congregational life.

No group of elders is perfect. All elders have weaknesses and each believer has a unique perspective on how elders should operate. As a result, there is always some degree of tension between leaders and followers. Even the best elders are accused of pride, wrong judgment, doing too much or too little, moving too slowly or too quickly, changing too much or not enough, and being too harsh or too passive. The exercise of authority is always apt to provoke resentment. Difficult situations sometimes arise in which leaders cannot avoid angering some part of the congregation. Conflict between leaders and the led can at times become severe. God sometimes uses these conflicts to show us our pride, selfishness and lovelessness.

Most controversies in local churches are produced not primarily by differences over essentials but by unsanctified human ambition, jealousy and personality clashes. The real root of many such situations is spiritual death in individual believers. The local church is one of the best laboratories in which individual believers may discover their real spiritual emptiness and begin to grow in love. This is done by true repentance. Believers who love their shepherds or leaders will have greater understanding and tolerance for their shepherd's mistakes. In love, believers will view difficult situations in the best possible light. In love, believers will be less critical and more responsive to the elders' instructions and admonitions. The best thing a congregation can do for its leaders is to love them. Love suffers long. Love covers a multitude of sins.

Love and esteem are due leaders "because of their work." Leaders are not to be loved and esteemed because they are older men, hold special religious titles or have nice personalities. Rather, they are to be loved "because of their work." Caring for people's problems, handling their seemingly endless complaints, refereeing conflicts, confronting sins and encouraging people toward maturity are all tough jobs. Few people are able or even care to bear the responsibility. Those who do it certainly deserve to be loved.

CHAPTER X

THE BIBLICAL STANDARDS FOR CHURCH LEADERSHIP

In addition to the apostolic requirement for eldership, it is important to understand the overall biblical standard that is required by God of church leadership. This chapter gives a much clearer view and understanding of this required standard for any form of leadership in the church.

The biblical standards for church leadership are personal character qualities, not college or seminary degrees, business administrative skills or personal charisma. We may tend to select our leaders on the basis of personal success or social standing, but Paul said to search deeper, to look for character qualities that reveal a deep-seated faith and reflect integrity, maturity and stability. The standards for elders, deacons or any form of leadership in the local church are high because they are to be "examples to the flock" (I Peter 5:3). And because leaders are in a position of responsibility, they are to be good examples of what it means to grow in Christ-likeness.

The biblical standards for church leaders are, for the most part, characteristics of a person who is taking his faith in Christ seriously, growing in his knowledge of God and maturing in his Christian life. In selecting church leaders, the criteria should be different from the way the world selects their leaders. Politicking, boasting, power games and popularity contests have no place in the church. Personal character and spiritual maturity should be the key issues for the selection of leaders.

Both elders and deacons have a direct influence on the spiritual well-being of the congregation. It is not surprising, then, that the Scriptures list a number of specific spiritual qualifications as the biblical standards for church leadership. The most extensive list of qualifications for leaders is found in I Timothy 3:1-13 and Titus 1:5-9. The requirements are more extensive for elders than for deacons. Both elders and deacons are to be "blameless" in character. The main difference in qualifications is that elders are expected to be "able to teach" and able "to exhort and convict" (Titus 1:9). Some qualifications for elders deal more particularly with their ability to relate well with people both in communicating the truth and in handling disagreements. In this chapter, as we stated earlier, we will combine the lists of qualifications and point out significant differences between the requirements for the two types of church leaders.

A Good Reputation

An old maxim states, "A chain is only as strong as its weakest link." That certainly is true when applied to the reputation of church leaders. A man may have great talents and an extensive knowledge of the truths of the Bible, but if his life has a "weak link," his reputation will suffer great damage and his ministry will be diminished, if not destroyed completely. That is why this first group of qualifications is so vital to leadership.

> **An overseer, then, must be above reproach, the husband of one wife, temperate, prudent, respectable, hospitable, able to teach,**
>
> **And let these also first be tested; then let them serve as deacons if they are beyond reproach.**
>
> **I Timothy 3:2, 10 NASB**
>
> **namely, if any man be above reproach, the husband of one wife, having children who believe, not accused of dissipation or rebellion.**
>
> **For the overseer must be above reproach as God's steward, not self-willed, not quick-tempered, not addicted to wine, not pugnacious, not fond of sordid gain,**
>
> **Titus 1:6, 7 NASB**

(1) *Blameless.* This is an all-inclusive quality relating to all areas of life. It is important that an elder, a deacon or a leader be above reproach in any of the important areas of personal character listed in I Timothy 3 or Titus 1. When tested, they must be found "blameless" in the sight of the people they will be ministering to. Does this mean that a man has to be perfect to be a church leader? Obviously not, since no one is perfect. But the characteristic pattern of his life must be in line with the biblical standards of leadership. Any leader who violates any one of these high standards must be dealt with speedily and biblically (Matthew 18:15-17, I Timothy 5:19-20). When considering a candidate, it should

be asked if there are any verifiable, unresolved charges of wrongdoing that could be brought against him.

> **And he must have a good reputation with those outside the church, so that he may not fall into reproach and the snare of the devil.**
>
> **I Timothy 3:7 NASB**

(2) *A good testimony among those outside.* Those "outside" are non-Christians who observe the testimony of church leaders. An elder cannot function effectively as a leader and witness in the community if a cloud of disgrace hangs over him because of questionable or clearly sinful activity. The witness of the entire church in the community and the authority of such a leader within the church itself would be seriously damaged by a bad reputation. If a leader's character is in question, it is not only bad for the church, but also dangerous for the individual. I Timothy 3:7 states that if an elder does not have a good reputation, he will fall into "the snare of the devil." Satan is working to discredit Christian leaders and to stifle the church's witness.

> **A bishop then must be blameless, the husband of one wife, vigilant, sober, of good behaviour, given to hospitality, apt to teach;**
>
> **I Timothy 3:2 KJV**

(3) *Of good behavior.* The word translated "of good behavior" can also be translated "respectable" or "honorable." It comes from the Greek word for "orderly" or "well-arranged." A man who likes an orderly life is conducting himself in an honorable manner, thus earning the respect of those around him. A leader should not be someone who runs from crisis to crisis because of his own disorganization. Any

candidate for church office should be observed and questioned to determine if his life reflects consistency and order.

> **Deacons likewise must be men of dignity, not double-tongued, or addicted to much wine or fond of sordid gain,**
>
> **I Timothy 3:8 NASB**

(4) *Reverent.* A person who serves in an official role in the church is to be respectable and dignified. Such an individual is to take his role seriously. Does the person have a frivolous attitude toward spiritual issues? Like the preceding characteristic, "of good behavior," would an observer, whether in or out of the church, respect the person and his official role?

Self Control

An addict is a person who has lost control of his life. The controlling factor may be cocaine, alcohol, food, sex, TV, anger, money, power, work or any all-consuming hobby. In each case, the person is controlled instead of being the controller. In contrast, a church leader is to exhibit self control. But what does it mean to be self-controlled?

> **but hospitable, loving what is good, sensible, just, devout, self-controlled,**
>
> **Titus 1:8 NASB**

(1) *Self-controlled.* A leader is to exhibit a disciplined life. He must demonstrate a growing Christ-likeness and be in control of his passions and appetites (Galatians 5:16-26). This self control is not self effort. It is cooperating with the

indwelling Spirit to make wise choices and to live in dependence upon Him. A self-controlled person chooses to live for God instead of self. His life is in order. He is not in bondage to sinful impulses. The following characteristics are a good indicator of a person's degree of self control.

> **Not given to wine, no striker, not greedy of filthy lucre; but patient, not a brawler, not covetous;**
>
> **Likewise must the deacons be grave, not doubletongued, not given to much wine, not greedy of filthy lucre;**
>
> **I Timothy 3:3, 8 KJV**
>
> **For a bishop must be blameless, as the steward of God; not selfwilled, not soon angry, not given to wine, no striker, not given to filthy lucre;**
>
> **Titus 1:7 KJV**

(2) *Not given to wine.* The Greek word used in I Timothy 3:3 and Titus 1:7 refers to a habit of overdrinking. In classical and Hellenistic times, the term had the meaning of being "tipsy" or "rowdy." The Greek word used in I Timothy 3:8 meant "to be attached to" or "addicted to" wine. Paul warns against the overindulgence of wine. That is, becoming known as someone who gets drunk or spends too much time drinking. Such a person would not be a worthy example, for he would fall into the danger of being controlled by wine instead of by the Spirit (Ephesians 5:18). A person being considered for leadership should be evaluated by these questions. Is his testimony diminished by a use of alcohol? Does he have a personal dependence on alcohol or drugs? Does he have any kind of addiction?

not given to drunkenness, not violent but gentle, not quarrelsome, not a lover of money.

I Timothy 3:3 NIV

(3) *Not quarrelsome.* An elder should not be a person commonly given to argument, disputation, controversy and rivalry. A mature person should be able to compromise on nonessential matters. When considering a candidate, ask these kinds of questions: Does the person find it difficult to participate in a dialogue if his point of view is not prevailing? Does he stubbornly maintain his viewpoint in the face of reasonable and unanswered objections?

For the overseer must be above reproach as God's steward, not self-willed, not quick-tempered, not addicted to wine, not pugnacious, not fond of sordid gain,

Titus 1:7 NASB

(4) *Not self-willed.* A person who is overbearing and inconsiderate is not qualified for leadership. Neither is someone who consistently displays an insensitive desire to have his way, regardless of facts, circumstances and the needs or feelings of people.

The questions to ask, then, are these: Does the person insist on always "being right?" Is he rude in his behavior when someone challenges his viewpoint? Does he resist worthy causes merely because he did not originate the idea?

For the overseer must be above reproach as God's steward, not self-willed, not quick-tempered, not

addicted to wine, not pugnacious, not fond of sordid gain,

Titus 1:7 NASB

(5) *Not quick-tempered.* A quick-tempered man becomes angry and belligerent very easily. Does the person being considered for leadership typically become so filled with emotion when facing opposition that he expresses himself in an angry, intimidating manner?

Deacons likewise must be men of dignity, not double-tongued, or addicted to much wine or fond of sordid gain,

I Timothy 3:8 NASB

(6) *Not double-tongued.* A church leader should be a person whose word can be trusted. He cannot be inconsistent or insincere in what he says. He cannot say one thing to one person and something contradictory to another. His yes means yes and his no means no. Is the person who is being considered for church office a man who keeps his promises? Or is he hypocritical in speech? Does he alter truth to serve his own best interests? Does he slander people behind their backs?

Godly Values

Would you be devastated if a thief stole your VCR and your television? How would you react if your life savings vanished with an investment broker? Do you spend more time washing your car than talking with your family? Does your occupation consume all of your thoughts and energy? Do you take time to pray and read the Bible? What does your checkbook or your credit card statement say about your values? These are the kinds of questions that reveal what we treasure most in life. Leadership is to show us what God values by what they value.

> **not addicted to wine or pugnacious, but gentle, uncontentious, free from the love of money.**
>
> **Deacons likewise must be men of dignity, not double-tongued, or addicted to much wine or fond of sordid gain,**
>
> **I Timothy 3:3, 8 NASB**
>
> **For the overseer must be above reproach as God's steward, not self-willed, not quick-tempered, not addicted to wine, not pugnacious, not fond of sordid gain,**
>
> **Titus 1:7 NASB**

(1) *Not greedy for money.* The priorities of a leader must not be centered on the accumulation of worldly wealth. He must be a good illustration of one who, though he may be wealthy, places his greatest priority on laying up treasures in heaven (Matthew 6:19-24). No one should be able to accuse a leader of using his position for personal financial gain (I Thessalonians 2:5). In his financial dealings, whether personal or business, he cannot be one who uses unethical or questionable tactics to make money.

> **Not given to wine, no striker, not greedy of filthy lucre; but patient, not a brawler, not covetous;**
>
> **I Timothy 3:3 KJV**

(2) *Not covetous.* This characteristic is closely related to "not greedy for money." A leader cannot be preoccupied with material wealth. The love of money leads a person away from

the faith (I Timothy 6:10). Several questions will help to discover if the candidate for leadership is greedy or covetous. Does he give more attention to things or to people? Is too much of his time involved in acquiring or maintaining material possessions?

> **but hospitable, loving what is good, sensible, just, devout, self-controlled,**

> ### Titus 1:8 NASB

(3) *A lover of what is good.* A lover of what is good means, "loving goodness." It refers to a person who "desires to do good, not evil." In Galatians 6:10, the apostle Paul stated, "Therefore, as we have opportunity, let us do good to all, especially to those who are of the household of faith." A lover of what is good means that such a person shows by his actions that he desires to reflect God's goodness in all that he does and in all of his relationships. He has the best interests of others in mind.

> **Rather he must be hospitable, one who loves what is good, who is self-controlled, upright, holy and disciplined.**

> ### Titus 1:8 NIV

(4) *Holy.* A leader must have an earnest desire to be pleasing to God. His attitude and actions must reflect a devoutness— a devotion to God. He must place a high priority on spiritual reality in his own life. His life should demonstrate that his heart is centered on God and His kingdom, not on worldly things. These characteristics may seem to be somewhat difficult to measure, but answering the following questions should help. Does the person's way of life and his conversation show that he takes God and His

Word seriously? Does the person set aside time for the study of Scripture and prayer?

A Loving Heart

In I Corinthians 13, the apostle Paul extolled the supremacy that love should have as a characteristic of our lives. It is no wonder, then, that Paul included several requirements that are indicative of a candidate's love for others. It is not enough for a leader to have a good knowledge of Scripture, be an effective teacher, give large sums of money to the church or ever profess great faith. Without love, it all adds up to nothing. The following qualifications are various aspects of how a leader is to express love.

> **not addicted to wine or pugnacious, but gentle, uncontentious, free from the love of money.**
>
> **I Timothy 3:3 NASB**

(1) *Gentle.* The exact meaning of this term is much broader than that which can be expressed with one word. All of the following terms approximate the meaning of the original Greek word: gracious, kind, forbearing, considerate, magnanimous, and genial. If a man is short-tempered, inconsiderate, rude or cruel, he would not be qualified for leadership.

> **not given to drunkenness, not violent but gentle, not quarrelsome, not a lover of money.**
>
> **I Timothy 3:3 NIV**

(2) *Not violent.* Literally, the Greek word means, "not a striker." A leader cannot be one who resorts to displays of temper or intimidation in order to control others. Nor does he

walk around with "a chip on his shoulder," looking for someone to knock it off. He does not seek to settle his differences of opinion with violent words or actions. Leadership must not be people who would make the leadership meeting a place for vicious verbal combat.

> **An overseer, then, must be above reproach, the husband of one wife, temperate, prudent, respectable, hospitable, able to teach,**
>
> **I Timothy 3:2 NASB**
>
> **but hospitable, loving what is good, sensible, just, devout, self-controlled,**
>
> **Titus 1:8 NASB**

(3) *Hospitable.* This term literally means, "loving strangers." In New Testament times, this quality referred to the action of befriending and giving lodging to fellow believers who were traveling or were fleeing persecution because of their faith in Christ. In a broader sense, to be hospitable refers to friendliness and a willingness to help others who need assistance.

A Healthy Home

Would you hire an auto mechanic who drives a sputtering, smoking pile of rusting junk? Or would you ask a dental hygienist with decayed teeth to instruct you on how to keep your teeth in good condition? Would you want a person who has been in five auto accidents in the last year to give you some driving tips?

We expect the person with whom we entrust our possessions and our lives to have some proven expertise, to know what he is talking about. The same is true of those in leadership. They must practice what they preach and be good examples to the believers they are guiding and serving. A person's home life is the most revealing aspect of his character and leadership ability. That is why Paul, in the lists he presents in I Timothy and in Titus, gives four qualifications that deal with the spiritual health of the leader's home.

> **An overseer, then, must be above reproach, the husband of one wife, temperate, prudent, respectable, hospitable, able to teach,**

> **Let deacons be husbands of only one wife, and good managers of their children and their own households.**

> ### I Timothy 3:2, 12 NASB

> **namely, if any man be above reproach, the husband of one wife, having children who believe, not accused of dissipation or rebellion.**

> ### Titus 1:6 NASB

(1) *He is the husband of one wife.* This qualification requires that if a leader is married, he must be faithfully devoted to his wife. Is the candidate a man who is dedicated to only one woman? A man who keeps a mistress or a flirtatious person clearly would not be qualified as a leader.

> **He must be one who manages his own household well, keeping his children under control with all dignity**

> **Let deacons be husbands of only one wife, and good managers of their children and their own households.**

> **I Timothy 3:4, 12 NASB**

(2) *He manages his house well.* Paul made the observation that a man who cannot govern his own household can hardly be trusted to govern the church. His children should be properly trained, and he must have a good relationship with his wife. This qualification may also include financial management. As the head of the family, a man must demonstrate the characteristics that will make him a fitting leader for a congregation. This does not mean that a leader is a perfect home manager, but it does require an affirmative answer to the question: Does he do a good job of managing his own household?

> **He must be one who manages his own household well, keeping his children under control with all dignity**

> **I Timothy 3:4 NASB**

> **namely, if any man be above reproach, the husband of one wife, having children who believe, not accused of dissipation or rebellion.**

> **Titus 1:6 NASB**

(3) *His children are obedient and respectful.* This is a more specific statement of how a leader is supposed to manage his own house. His children are to show evidence that their father is a respected leader at home and that he knows how to instruct and discipline them. No father has perfect children, so we should not expect perfection from the children of leaders. But, as Titus 1:6 states, the children

should behave in such a way that no one can accuse them of being wild or insubordinate.

> **namely, if any man be above reproach, the husband of one wife, having children who believe, not accused of dissipation or rebellion.**

> **Titus 1:6 NASB**

(4) *His children are believers.* This qualification is specifically required of leadership because of their responsibility for the spiritual welfare of their congregation. This qualification does not demand that the leaders' children act like little angels all the time, but it does mean that they profess their faith in Christ.

A Mature Faith

If you wanted to learn how to fly an airplane, what kind of teacher would you prefer: a 9 year old who builds model airplanes, or a licensed and tested flight instructor with thousands of hours of actual flying time? Who should be leading our local churches and instructing believers in how to live the Christian life? For obvious reasons, we would prefer to have leaders who have a proven and steady faith— a faith that is experienced and mature.

> **Not a novice, lest being lifted up with pride he fall into the condemnation of the devil.**

> **I Timothy 3:6 KJV**

(1) *Not a novice.* A candidate for leadership position is not to be a new convert. A new believer has not earned a good reputation as a Christian. He is not known well enough in the Christian community. The apostle Paul warned that if

an immature believer were quickly elevated to a position of leadership, he would be in danger of becoming proud and "fall into the same condemnation as the devil" (I Timothy 3:6). That is, he would be filled with the same kind of pride that led to Satan's fall and be subject to God's judgment. Advancing a new Christian too rapidly could lead to his having an inflated, unrealistic assessment of his spiritual condition. Even though a candidate may fulfill many of the other qualifications, it is very important to investigate whether he has enough Christian experience to be humble if he were to be elevated to the position of leadership.

And let these also first be tested; then let them serve as deacons if they are beyond reproach.

I Timothy 3:10 NASB

(2) *Tested.* A leader should not be a novice. He must be a person of maturity in faith and character. He must have shown by his faithfulness that he is qualified for official service. Has the individual demonstrated his ability to function as an example to others? Is his life in harmony with the scriptural qualifications? These are some of the questions that must be answered.

but holding to the mystery of the faith with a clear conscience.

I Timothy 3:9 NASB

(3) *Hold the mystery of the faith with a clear conscience.* A leader cannot be a hypocrite. His faith cannot be merely intellectual, contradicting his day-to-day pattern of living. He must display a sincerity of faith and a firm conviction of the truth of God's Word.

> **holding fast the faithful word which is in accordance with the teaching, that he may be able both to exhort in sound doctrine and to refute those who contradict.**

> **Titus 1:9 NASB**

(4) *Holding fast the faithful word.* A leader is required to be one who has a firm grounding in sound doctrine. They must be convinced of its truthfulness and be willing and able to defend it. When considering a person for leadership, ask these questions: Does the person base his lifestyle and decisions on the written Word of God? Does he respect the Scriptures as the final word of authority in all matters of faith, life and practice? Or does he exhibit a tendency to ignore or bypass biblical absolutes?

> **holding fast the faithful word which is in accordance with the teaching, that he may be able both to exhort in sound doctrine and to refute those who contradict.**

> **Titus 1:9 NASB**

(5) *Able to exhort and convince.* A person that is placed in leadership, especially an elder, must be "able to teach." He should be a man who knows the Bible well. He should have a firm handle on the truth and be able to explain convincingly the demands of Scripture on our lives. When confronted by a person who is wrapped up in false doctrine, would he be able to recognize the error? Would he also be able to discuss appropriate Scripture passages that speak to the issue?

A Teachable Mind

Some people can be as stubborn as a mule. No matter how you reason with them, they refuse to listen. Once they make up their mind, they don't want to be confused with the facts. When such a person is appointed to a leadership position in the church, trouble is soon to follow. A leader must be able to discuss conflicting ideas and come to wise decisions. That is why the apostle Paul listed several characteristics of a qualified leader that reflect the ability to think objectively.

All of the qualities in this section are required character traits for leadership and for good reason. Leaders are to be the key decision-makers in the church. They have the primary responsibility for proclaiming and protecting the truth as well as dealing with the many details of church life.

> **An overseer, then, must be above reproach, the husband of one wife, temperate, prudent, respectable, hospitable, able to teach,**
>
> **I Timothy 3:2 NASB**

(1) *Able to teach.* This is a key qualification with two shades of meaning. First, it means that a leader must be able to instruct others regarding biblical truth. But the Greek word can also mean, "teachable." Most likely, there is more implied here than just the ability to teach. In the context, this quality seems to refer to an ability to communicate the truth without arrogance. A leader should be willing to be corrected. The best teachers are those who see themselves as communicators of truth, not the originators of it. An open-minded, reasonable spirit is an essential quality of leadership, as is a recognition of the importance of dialogue.

The following questions will help to evaluate a candidate: Does the individual have a firm grasp of biblical truth? Is he able to explain that truth to others? Does he have a mind that is open to new information, even if it runs contrary to his current opinions? Does he possess the ability to discuss any issue in an objective and patient manner?

> **An overseer, then, must be above reproach, the husband of one wife, temperate, prudent, respectable, hospitable, able to teach,**
>
> **I Timothy 3:2 NASB**

(2) *Temperate.* This word means more than just moderation in eating or drinking. Gene Getz states that, "a man who is temperate does not lose his physical, psychological, and spiritual orientation. He remains stable and steadfast, and his thinking is clear." He is balanced in his living, not prone to destructive extremes.

When considering a person for church leadership, we should ask if the individual shows a reliable sense of balance in his judgment. Does he exhibit any tendency toward fanaticism or legalism, which could interfere with the effectiveness of his overall judgment and ministry?

> **An overseer, then, must be above reproach, the husband of one wife, temperate, prudent, respectable, hospitable, able to teach,**
>
> **I Timothy 3:2 NASB**
>
> **but hospitable, loving what is good, sensible, just, devout, self-controlled,**
>
> **Titus 1:8 NASB**

(3) *Sober minded.* The meaning of this word is very closely related to the previous term, temperate. A leader that is leading God's people must be sensible in his thinking and actions. He cannot be someone who is prone to act on impulse or make rash and irrational decisions. He must be self-controlled and prudent in his actions. A true leader avoids quick decisions based on inadequate information, and he generally exhibits sound judgment.

> **but hospitable, loving what is good, sensible, just, devout, self-controlled,**
>
> **Titus 1:8 NASB**

(4) *Just.* A person who exercises authority in the church must be concerned with justice in all his dealings. He must do what is right and be fair in all situations. A leader therefore must have the courage to seek truth, even when it is inconvenient or controversial. He always seeks to be fair and impartial. And he must seek to make decisions on the basis of principle, not personalities.

CHAPTER XI

HOW TO SET UP AN ELDERSHIP TEAM IN A LOCAL CHURCH

And when they had appointed elders for them in every church, having prayed with fasting, they commended them to the Lord in whom they had believed.

Acts 14:23 NASB

One of the highly misunderstood processes in the Church is the process that involves setting elders apart for their assignments. Many churches fail in this area with the sad result that unfit or untested men are appointed as elders and qualified men are never developed or properly recognized. All elders that lead God's people are to be fully qualified, formally examined and publicly installed into office. There are biblical processes for appointing elders and these processes must not be set aside. Some of these processes or elements involve the individual's desire, his qualifications, the selection itself, the individual examination, his installation and prayer.

It is a trustworthy statement: if any man aspires to the office of overseer, it is a fine work he desires to do.

I Timothy 3:1 NASB

Let the elders who rule well be considered worthy of double honor, especially those who work hard at preaching and teaching.

I Timothy 5:17 NASB

For the overseer must be above reproach as God's steward, not self-willed, not quick-tempered, not addicted to wine, not pugnacious, not fond of sordid gain,

Titus 1:7 NASB

The Bible makes it clear that a local church should have overseers. Overseers supervise the activities of the local church. The Scripture says in I Timothy 5:17 that the elders are the ones who "rule" the local church. The word "rule" here is the Greek word *prohistemi* which means, "lead, manage or direct." So when it comes to the setting apart of appointment of elders, it is very important that the overseers of that local church supervise and direct the entire process of selecting, examining, approving and installing prospective elders.

In all New Testament cases of initial elder or deacon appointments, the apostles or an apostolic delegate initiated and supervised the appointment process. If the elders or the overseers do not oversee or supervise the process, disorder and mismanagement will take place and people will be hurt. The elders have the authority, the position and the knowledge to move the church to action. They know the needs of the church and the people.

Even though the New Testament did not show any examples of elders appointing elders, perpetuation of the eldership is implied in the elders' role as congregational shepherds, stewards and overseers. It is absolutely vital that the elders of a local church recognize the Spirit-given desire of others to shepherd the flock. If an individual desires to be an elder and truly exhibits that desire through appropriate action, and if he is morally qualified, then the present elders are obligated to see that such a person is not frustrated in his desire.

And the things which you have heard from me in the presence of many witnesses, these entrust to faithful men, who will be able to teach others also.

II Timothy 2:2 NASB

Solid eldership teams are constantly praying and looking for capable men to join them and are conscientiously training and preparing men for future leadership. In the above Scripture, Paul told Timothy that, "the things which you have heard from me in the presence of many witnesses, these entrust or commit to faithful men who will be able to teach others also." Ideally, long before the church examines a prospective elder, such an individual will have prepared himself and will have been trained by the elders and watched by the congregation. This makes the process move faster.

The Appointment Process

The New Testament says very little concerning such detailed procedures as appointing elders. In the same way, the New Testament is amazingly silent regarding special procedures for administering the Lord's supper and baptism. Exact procedures for these activities are left to the discretion of the local church. Even under the Mosaic law, which prescribed detailed regulations for every area of life, matters such as appointment and organization of elders were left to the people's discretion. God expects the saints to use the creativity and wisdom He has given to organize all such matters within the revealed guidelines of His Word. Although the New Testament did not provide a clear blueprint for the process of eldership appointment, it specifies certain key principles: The desire principle, the qualifications principle, the selection principle, the installation and prayer principle.

The Desire Principle

It is a trustworthy statement: if any man aspires to the office of overseer, it is a fine work he desires to do.

And by common confession great is the mystery of godliness: He who was revealed in the flesh, Was vindicated in the Spirit, Beheld by angels, Proclaimed among the nations, Believed on in the world, Taken up in glory.

I Timothy 3:1, 16 NASB

Be on guard for yourselves and for all the flock, among which the Holy Spirit has made you overseers, to shepherd the church of God which He purchased with His own blood.

Acts 20:28 NASB

The first principle to consider in appointing elders is the individual's personal desire. The desire to be an elder is not sinful or self-promoting, if it is generated by God's Spirit. Paul reminded the Ephesian elders that it was the Holy Spirit who had placed them in the congregation as elders. This means, among other things, that it was the Holy Spirit who planted in the hearts of the elders the desire and motivation to be elders. Peter also addresses the need for an elder to shepherd God's flock with a willing heart. So the starting point is a Spirit given desire to be a shepherd of God's people.

A Spirit given desire for eldership will naturally demonstrate itself in action. It cannot be held in. A man who desires to be an elder will let others know of his desire. That is one way in which the congregation and elders can know of a prospective elder. The knowledge of this desire will prompt the elders to pray and to encourage such desire through appropriate training and leadership development. More important, the person with a Spirit created motivation for the work of eldership will devote much time, thought and energy to caring for people and studying the Scriptures. There is no such thing as a Spirit given desire for eldership or leadership without the corresponding evidence of sacrificial, loving service and love for God's Word. Eldership or leadership is a strenuous task, not just another position on a decision-making board. In fact, the stronger a man's desire for eldership, the stronger will be his leadership and love for people and the Word.

But we request of you, brethren, that you appreciate those who diligently labor among you, and have charge over you in the Lord and give you instruction,

I Thessalonians 5:12 NASB

That means that before the candidate begins desiring an eldership position, he or she is already proving himself by leading, teaching and bearing responsibility in the church. In the above Scriptures, Paul reminds the congregation of its responsibility to acknowledge and recognize those in the congregation who work hard at leading and instructing others. One way the church acknowledges a man's diligent labors is to recommend and encourage him to prepare for eldership.

The Selection and Examination Process

And let these also first be tested; then let them serve as deacons if they are beyond reproach.

I Timothy 3:10 NASB

The sins of some men are quite evident, going before them to judgment; for others, their sins follow after.

Likewise also, deeds that are good are quite evident, and those which are otherwise cannot be concealed.

I Timothy 5:24-25 NASB

In selecting prospective elders, the examination of their moral and spiritual fitness for the office must be taken very seriously. A formal and public examination of a prospective elder's qualifications must be looked into. In I Timothy 3:10, Paul says, "And let these (deacons) also (like the elders) first be tested; then let them serve as deacons if they are beyond reproach." I Timothy 5:24-25 also teaches that an assessment of character and deeds is necessary in order to avoid appointing the wrong people as elders or overlooking qualified men.

First of all, then, I urge that entreaties and prayers, petitions and thanksgivings, be made on behalf of all men,

I Timothy 2:1 NASB

And by common confession great is the mystery of godliness: He who was revealed in the flesh, Was

118

vindicated in the Spirit, Beheld by angels, Proclaimed among the nations, Believed on in the world, Taken up in glory.

I Timothy 3:16 NASB

Although the elders are supposed to take the lead in all church procedures, that does not mean the congregation is passive. True elders want an informed, involved congregation. Biblical elders eagerly desire to listen to, consult with and seek the wisdom of their fellow believers. The prospective elder or deacon will serve the congregation, so the people must have a voice in examining and approving their prospective elders and deacons. The context in which I Timothy 3:10 appears lays out general instructions for the whole church, not just for the elders. Everyone in the church is to know the biblical qualifications for church elders and is obligated to see that the elders meet those qualifications. Some people in a congregation may have information about a prospective elder or deacon that the elders do not have, so their input in the evaluation process is absolutely essential, regardless of how that process is carried out in detail.

Objections and Accusations

If there are objections and accusations that are voiced about a candidate's character, the elders must investigate to determine if the accusations or objection are Scripturally-based. If not, the objections or accusations should be dismissed. No individual should be refused or rejected because of someone's personal bias. Members of the congregation must give Scriptural reasons for their objections. This examination process is not a popularity contest or church election. It is an assessment of a candidate's character according to the Scripture.

Checking Doctrinal Beliefs

During a meeting or several meetings with the prospective leader, the elders and the congregation should inquire about the prospective candidate's doctrinal beliefs, personal giftedness, ministry interests, family unity, moral integrity, and commitment of time. The prospective leader must be examined regarding his knowledge and ability to use the Word to counsel people and direct the church. For example, the candidate should be able to open the Bible and answer questions such as: What does the Bible teach about divorce and remarriage? Where in the Bible does it teach Christ's divine nature? What does the Bible say about male and female roles? What does the Bible say about church discipline? and many more doctrinal issues.

Members of the congregation must be given the opportunity to either verbally or in written form express freely their questions, doubts or approval of a candidate for eldership. Finally, the elders as the chief representatives and stewards of the local church will formally state in full consultation with the church their approval, rejection, reservations or counsel concerning the prospective elder.

The Installation Process

And let these also first be tested; then let them serve as deacons if they are beyond reproach.

I Timothy 3:10 NASB

After the selection and examination process and the elders' final approval, the candidate should be publicly installed into office. The word "first" in the above Scripture tells us that there is an order to observe when appointing elders or deacons or any form of leader. An individual desiring eldership, deaconship or any form of leadership position must first be examined. Only after he is shown to be biblically qualified can he then be installed into office. The New Testament provides little detailed instruction about the elders' public installation into office and the Old Testament says nothing about it.

New Testament elders, deacons or leaders are not anointed priests like Aaron and his sons. Elders, deacons and leaders are not appointed to a special priestly office or holy clerical order. They are just assuming offices of leadership or service among God's people. There is no holy rite to perform or special ceremony to observe. Appointment to eldership is not a holy sacrament. Appointment confers no special grace or empowerment to become a priest or a cleric at the moment of installation.

The Prayer Process

They have set up kings, but not by Me; They have appointed princes, but I did not know it. With their silver and gold they have made idols for themselves, That they might be cut off.

Hosea 8:4 NASB

The final process is that all procedures concerning the appointment of elders, deacons and leaders must be bathed in "heavy" prayer. The church and its leaders must pray for Scriptural insight, guidance, and unbiased judgment. They must desire God's will and God's choice and not their own. In Hosea 8:4, God told Israel, "they have set up kings, but not by me, they have appointed princes, but I did not know it." May God not say that of us. Sadly, many churches expend little amount of time and effort when selecting and examining prospective eldership, deaconship or leadership candidates. Thoughtless, lazy and prayerless procedures weaken a church and demean the eldership, the deaconship and the leadership.

Do not lay hands upon anyone too hastily and thus share responsibility for the sins of others; keep yourself free from sin.

I Timothy 5:22 NASB

Evaluating the fitness of an elder, deacon or leader for office must be done thoughtfully, patiently and biblically. The Scripture clearly states that no one is to be appointed to any office in a hurried, thoughtless manner. Once a man is appointed to the eldership and deaconship position, he serves as long as he desires, functions in the work and remains qualified. It is unscriptural, harmful to the church and demeaning to the elders to set limits on the time period an elder or a deacon can serve.

CHAPTER XII

THE RELATIONSHIP BETWEEN ELDERSHIP TEAMS AND THE CONGREGATIONS

and that you esteem them very highly in love because of their work. Live in peace with one another.

I Thessalonians 5:13 NASB

In the local church there are no rulers who sit above or subjects who stand below. All are equally brothers and sisters in the church family, although some function as Spirit placed overseers to authoritatively guide and protect the church family. As leaders, elders are under the strict authority of Jesus Christ and His Holy Word. They cannot do or say whatever they want. The Church does not belong to the elders. It belongs to God. It is Christ's Church. That is why leadership is to be exercised in a way that models Christ-like, humble, loving leadership.

Submission is always difficult. Our hearts are stubborn, prideful and rebellious. Yet we are called to submit, even in trying and disagreeable situations. Children must submit to imperfect parents, wives to difficult husbands and employees to demanding employers. Likewise, the congregation is required to submit to and obey its elders, even if the elders have weaknesses and faults. Sure, elders have some form of imperfection, so those who are disobedient can always find reason to revolt. Sometimes the things we consider to be the elders' misjudgment or errors may well be our own errors. We must not be too hasty to disregard the judgment of those God has chosen to provide for our spiritual care.

The requirement to submit, however, is not meant to suggest blind, mindless submission. Nor does it suggest that elders are above questioning or exempt from public discipline. The elders are most assuredly answerable to the congregation, and the congregation is responsible to hold its spiritual leaders accountable to faithful adherence to the truth of the Word. Members have a voice in assuring that what is done in the church family is done according to Scripture. So there is a tightly knit, delicate and reciprocal relationship between elders and congregation.

The goal of the elders and congregation should always be to speak and act as a united community. Both the leaders and the led should take the time and make the effort needed to work and pray together to achieve this oneness of mind. This means that elders must inoculate themselves against secrecy or independently seeking their own direction. Godly eldership teams desire to involve every member of the body in the joy of living together as the family of God. This requires a great deal of free and open communication between the elders and congregation.

The first Christian congregation provides us with an example of a leadership council and congregation working together in decision making and problem solving. In Acts 6, when conflict broke out between the Hebrew and Hellenistic widows in the congregation over the fair distribution of funds, the Twelve (the leadership council) immediately devised a plan for resolving the problem. They called the congregation together and presented their plans. The congregation approved the plan, which called for their participation in choosing seven men to take responsibility for the care of all the church widows. After the seven were chosen by the congregation, the apostles officially placed the seven men in charge of the poor by the laying on of hands and prayer.

> **And when they arrived at Jerusalem, they were received by the church and the apostles and the elders, and they reported all that God had done with them.**
>
> **But certain ones of the sect of the Pharisees who had believed, stood up, saying, "It is necessary to circumcise them, and to direct them to observe the Law of Moses."**
>
> **And the apostles and the elders came together to look into this matter.**

Acts 15:4-6 NASB

In the Scripture above, the congregation in Jerusalem was confronted with serious doctrinal controversy. The whole church in this situation was involved in resolving the controversy with the apostles and the elders taking the lead in all of the proceedings. The apostles and the elders permitted public debate. The apostles, who were the chief leaders within the leadership, resolved the matter so that all of the leaders and the people could become of one mind. They looked out among the congregation and chose deacons. The New Testament does not prescribe detailed rules and regulations regarding the elder/congregation relationship or decision making process. But it is absolutely clear in the New Testament that love, humility and prayer are to guide all of our relationships and decisions.

To request a complete catalog featuring books, video or audio tapes by Dr. John A. Tetsola, or to contact him for speaking engagements, please write or call:

Ecclesia Word Ministries International
P.O. Box 743
Bronx, New York 10462

(718) 904-8530
(718) 904-8107 fax
www.ecclesiaword.org
www.reformersministries.org
email: reformers@msn.com